Just Your Type:
How to Thrive in Relationships Using Personality Types and More

Christa Hardin, M.A.

Sharon Otis, Ph.D., Ed.D.

JUST YOUR TYPE

Just Your Type: *How to Thrive in Relationships Using Personality Types and More*

DEDICATION

We would not have this amazing opportunity to look at marriage and relationships nearly to the degree we can without our faithful husbands Wes and Dennis. They put up with our issues, love us through our faults, and love us as their brides to this day. We are so grateful to them and to God! We dedicate this book to them in love and to the legacy of love we will leave to those we love together.

JUST YOUR TYPE

Praise for *What's Your Type?*

It is my distinct honor and privilege to recommend the book "Just Your Type," written by two talented and effective clinicians who are also sisters in Christ. It is a step-by-step and concise guide in navigating relationships using personality testing and including male/female brain differences. The beauty of God's grace through trauma, infidelity and co-dependency issues is woven through the book. The Fifty Date Night ideas were like icing on a delicious cake! I know you will be glad you read it.

- Dr. Elizabeth John, MD, Psychiatrist

JUST YOUR TYPE

CONTENTS

JUST YOUR TYPE

Introduction

One of the first families I ever worked with is still vividly etched in my memory, even though that was almost eighteen years ago. I was an intern in Wheaton, Illinois, training with a wonderful not-for-profit Christian center that supports families through counseling, adoption services, foster care and pregnancy services. As a new therapist in the counseling division, I loved meeting this kind, though troubled, family. The husband, Dave, was a surgeon, and the wife Lisa was an early elementary teacher. Together they were a beautiful couple, and to the world, they certainly looked picture perfect, although this family was actually heartbroken. Their oldest child was struggling with severe social anxiety. In turn, they too were struggling with how to get him to come out of his shell and to be comfortable in the world.

I made a few early observations as they told me about their son's issues and in the intake process, I saw their non-verbal communication. My early theories not only acknowledged he may be on the autism spectrum or have anxiety issues, but also some family issues. Was Lisa coddling their son too much? Was Dave too brash or insensitive to his son's emotional needs? My early observations were soon confirmed with their frank and humble willingness to share their core personalities with me.

You see, as much as we need to pay attention to our heredity and environment, our personalities also cannot be overlooked as they influence everything we do. This couple was willing to look at how their own personality traits contributed to their son's gifts and struggles, even above and beyond their individual heredity, environmental and occupational triggers. This brave step, being willing to grow personally, was foundational for the healing of their family. Their inner reflection truly allowed them to learn how their own gifts and personalities contributed both to their son's health and to his struggles. More importantly, they realized what they could do to make the family system a healthier place for all.

As you may have guessed, they learned that Dave wasn't

naturally being interactive with their son and that Lisa was being overprotective, trying to smooth things out every step of the way. As a result the little boy felt frail and uncertain as a growing child, being overidentified with by sweet mom and largely emotionally ignored by dad. How many other little ones have grown up this way with well-meaning parents who were just a bit off course until a disaster woke them up?

Please don't despair over this. When individuals and couples work hard to use their gifts, their families become healthy, plain and simple. They don't need to reinvent the wheel, they don't need to enter years of intensive couples therapy, and they sure don't need to worry that it's too hard. They just need to take one small step forward each day, with a willingness to grow and to learn. With a few tools and practical skills, every person, couple, and family can learn to thrive. Though the names, personalities, and occupations change with each unique family we work with (and we have changed names and all identifying information in this book for privacy purposes), Sharon and I have seen so many other couples just like Dave and Lisa through our private practices. They're well-meaning, loving and caring, but sometimes a little (or a lot!) lost.

Sharon, who is an Ed.D. and Ph.D., psychotherapist co-writing this book with me, learned this important family truth years back when she was an educator in the school systems. She could help deserving children all day long but almost always, unless a parent or guardian got healthier in their relationships, their children simply would not thrive. Treating the family as a whole was so strong of a concern that she switched careers and has now been working as a therapist in private practice for many years. Sharon's great reputation of expertise in family systems work precedes her wherever she goes, which is how I heard of her years ago when I first moved to Florida.

Your Family Legacy

So what about your relationships? As you begin to grow as an individual by learning about your family's preferences, gifts, and personality types in this book, we are going to show you what to do each step of the way. And if you truly want to grow, we ask you to lay some of your preconceived notions aside, namely any desire to "show someone" how to be, or a desire to "fix" a spouse. Instead, we want you to look at this book as an opportunity for clear personal and family growth, which starts with an open mind and a nonjudgemental spirit.

If your desire is for a joyful, healthy and enriched marriage and family now (or in the years ahead if you're single), in this book, we will give you the tools for success that I gave that couple years ago in my early days of practice. But not only that, now you get the added eighteen years of practice since grad school. Combine that with Sharon's thirty five years, and we have a total of fifty-three years of tools and experience. That's obviously a lot, so if you put your focus on this, you WILL come out changed for the better on the other side. It is then possible for you to model healthy behavior too, and people will want what you have.

We are excited for you to courageously open up this bright new chapter of your life and legacy with us here. If you're still not convinced, we've bullet-pointed a few reasons you should complete this book along with a few key steps for success.

Why Should You Complete This Workbook?

If you're working on your marriage actively, you will learn to thrive as a couple with fun, relaxation, and emotional comfort. To put it simply, you'll enjoy life more together!

If you're working on this single, pre-marriage or in a dating relationship, you're going to learn about what your deepest needs are in a marriage and family relationship so you can target your biggest triggers and get past them. Relationships are not fifty-fifty to be healthy. They require one hundred percent each.

If you're a parent, you'll help current and future generations of children to thrive because you are moving into a position of health and offering a firm foundation for them. As J.R.R. Tolkien said, *"It is not our part to master all the tides of the world, but to do what is in us for the [help] of those years..., so that those who live after may have clean earth to till. What weather they shall have is not ours to rule."*

Because of the intentional simple but balanced self care steps we teach, you will have more wellness and wisdom for physical, emotional, financial, and especially spiritual stability now and as you lay groundwork for future generations.

You will approach life less from your shadow side or negative qualities and learn to apply and strengthen your gifts to get you through tough times and to make your goals both accessible and achievable.

How and When Should You Complete This Workbook?

Feel free to complete this book on your own. Family growth can begin even from one person's small steps in the family. As discouraging as it can feel to be intrinsically tied up with someone else who isn't willing to change, take heart. When you change, it causes movement in the family, which is a system. Because you shifted that system, someone else has to move forward or backward. Give the other(s) in your family, especially your spouse or partner, some grace and time to adjust to your moving and growing. Remember, this isn't about manipulating. Try to see them the way God sees them, broken but beloved.

You can also complete this with your partner if you're in a serious relationship or marriage. It's wonderful to experience growth both on your own and together. Again, some of your spouses or partners won't want to do this book and that's OK! Never force someone else's growth, you can only change you.

Complete this book on a daily or weekly basis. In our experience, many people like to read books cover to cover eagerly, but if you do this, your brain will overload you all at once so be sure to come back and take it week by week after you've done your initial read through. Ideally, you'll work on one module per week on your own time or with a semester study group.

After you're done reading, keep this book around as a reference tool for tough seasons. Sometimes relationships are effortless, and at other times and in other seasons, they're the most painful work and ministry you've ever done. Keep your workbook and tools around for times like this.

What Will You Learn in this Workbook?

We don't want to waste even one second of your valuable time, so we've streamlined the most important relationship topics into ten modules that you can complete all together as a couple, in a group, or individually depending on your need. Since each module has something in it for everyone, we recommend finding your way to each of them in time. Specifically, the things you'll learn in each module, or chapter, are:

Module 1: Building A Strong Foundation & Discovering Your Attachment Needs

Module 2: Understanding God's Good Plan for Your Broken Pieces

Module 3: Reclaiming Your Trauma

Module 4: Navigating Male and Female Brain Differences

Module 5: Understanding How Love Languages & Birth Order Influence Us

Module 6: Letting Go of Codependency in Your Relationships

Module 7: Adding Fun to Your Relationship + 50 Great Dates

Module 8: Navigating Unique Situational Challenges

Module 9: The Original Personality Typing - Discovering Your Temperament

Module 10: Finding Your Enneagram Personality Type

How Can You Use What You've Learned?

With our counseling, coaching and teaching backgrounds, we know that not only does it take reading to learn, but that it also takes doing. As such, we've included special questions for you to answer. Please take a moment to answer each question as it comes, just at face value. There is no right or wrong answer, but in order to grow and change, you do have to evaluate how you're doing things now so you can modify as needed. Remember to keep your phone nearby for writing in your *"Notes"* app, or take a pen and paper beside you. If this is a printed copy, we welcome you to write notes right in your workbook in the provided spaces and in the margins as well if you like.

As you begin the journey, you may also want to know that Sharon and I have not only put a lot of years into our work with couples, we've put a lot of heart and soul and prayer into our own families and marriages as well. We know how hard the work can be sometimes but we also know that these tools will yield a peaceful harvest, as we are reminded in Hebrews 12:11, *"No discipline seems pleasant at the time, but painful. Later on, however, it produces a harvest of righteousness and peace for those who have been trained by it."*

Even during our writing, the energy and commitment Sharon has put into her marriage was obvious to me, Christa. When I would go over to Sharon's home to write during this book project, I just loved seeing her actively playing with my children, her own grandchildren, or casually washing her therapy dog off after a swim. We worked from her beautiful canal-front lanai she and her husband worked very hard to obtain. More than anything, as a marriage helper, it was especially wonderful to see her and her husband, Dennis, interact. As an Enneagram 2 and 9, this is a fun couple! We'll get more into Enneagram type couples in Module 10 as we explore your own type!

Sharon and Dennis are so in sync because they have put plenty of love, commitment and devotion into their marriage to make sure it stays that way. They have differences that clash, like any couple, but the key is that they work with those differences to resolve them. Sharon says about this, *"At the beginning of marriage I would blame, react and awfulize, and now, in addition to knowing how my busy personality works, I take time to go to God in the morning and to listen to the Holy Spirit."*

As wonderful as Sharon's marriage looks, your healthy marriage may look entirely different from hers. If you see my husband and I enjoying our marriage, it looks very different from Sharon's. It may look like us cracking up laughing as we watch our favorite show, or sometimes you'll see us hiking, dancing the tango, reading a favorite passage together out of a book, or just quietly listening to music on a car date. Many times, in this busy stage with children at home, it looks a little like serving and teamwork, and that's because relationships are that as well.

At any rate, joy and peace look different on different people and in different stages. We learn in 1st Corinthians 12, which we will visit later, that the body of Christ is made up of interwoven parts. All of us have a role to play, but each of us has our own divine unique imprint and special gifting.

Our hope for this book is to bring you a richer understanding of the gifts you bring personally and also the strengths you bring to the world as a couple and as a family. It will be a huge blessing to you all as you learn to blend your beautiful gifts together!

Enjoy!

Christa and Sharon

MODULE 1: BUILDING A STRONG FOUNDATION & DISCOVERING YOUR ATTACHMENT NEEDS

I remember all the girls in my class saying they were going to marry a certain boy. The more assertive girls naturally hunted him down and had the weddings all planned out, down to the amount of children they would have together. We were all of five years old in kindergarten, and we were already vying for mates. Our needs obviously changed as we matured in our relationships, but it was telling of the personality types even then.

What is your earliest memory of relationship seeking? What do you think you were looking for as a child? Did this change as you evolved into a teen and then into an adult? Your thinking will change many times over with the formation of the frontal lobe of the brain and your own personality as it unfolds.

I wanted to marry Andrew briefly as well, but knew I, being quiet, was likely far down his list of prospects, so I tried to find others who were less likely to be taken but perhaps still marriage material. Apparently, another boy catching wind of this, blew into my ear in the lunch line. He was met with a cool slap on the cheek from me as he was definitely NOT the one.

Sharon's oldest granddaughter is almost seventeen and has been fortunate enough to avoid dating too young. One of the reasons for that is that she hasn't found a boy who meets her standards, so she is wisely waiting. It helps that one of her gifts is that she's sensitive to people who make bad decisions. She does not want to hang with kids who drink or break the law. Other teens have to find this out the hard way.

What was a red-flag to you that someone was not a good fit for you as you relationship searched?

_____

_____

_____

_____

As you think about what it is you're looking for in your own marriage or relationship, or a future one, make a brief list of relationship *"must haves"* and *"can't stands"* here or on a piece of paper. Many times, we marry our opposite so God will teach us how the other person can be the sandpaper that helps smooth out our weaknesses. Getting along with someone different teaches us about grace. *What do you need? If you're already married, what is it you feel you must have?*

_____

_____

_____

_____

As funny as it is to to think back on these old memories and the silly romance games that start ridiculously early for some of us, marriage is a lifelong dream for most of us. We know when it is the right timing for marriage when we know ourselves and what it is we're looking for, as well as what we need most to thrive. Sadly, some people spend more time picking out a cell phone plan or a car than on picking out their lifelong mate. We talk to our single clients, engaged or dating clients, children, grandchildren, friends, and nieces and nephews about looking at their potential mate from different perspectives, but many don't want to spend time waiting to do this. This is a grave mistake.

I'm lonely today, one says. Another says, *Waiting sounds good but it's painful.* We know. Even God in the Bible saw man alone and said it wasn't good. So what gives?

Whether you're currently married or reading this as a relationship guide for the future, you should know that there's certainly no universal time to marry. Some of the most successful couples have short but highly intentional courtships, while many doomed relationships have extensive ones. But overall, there's another factor we'd like you to consider before you say, "I do" for the first time or again. And that is whether you are personally ready.

To help figure that out, we've created six important R's before you say "I do." However, if you're already married, trust us, this list will be used to set things back on track and can be framed as a list of current #marriagegoals.

1. Realize you can be happy on your own even if you and your mate do not have the same interests.

You need to remember the mystery of marriage. Yes, you are one flesh, but you are not conjoined physically. If you BOTH want to be together all the time AND do all the same things enthusiastically, go for it (We find this with Enneagram 2's, 3's and 4's, those who lead with the heart, which we will talk about in Module 10). Otherwise, be ready to compromise and to give some space in hobbies and free time but keep a close connection and conversation going about these things.

2. Revisit your commitment to each other, even while seriously dating and especially if engaged or married.

If someone flirts with you, watch out especially if there is good chemistry, backing off and letting their flattery be instead a springboard of gratitude you bring into your day. Do not return the flirtation for anything.

Ask yourself now, do you have any temptations in your relationships that need to be addressed? Who can hold you accountable? Make sure to be open to your partner about it too, including the "why" of your attraction(s) elsewhere so you can grow together. Do you have anyone you need to let go of? We will visit this more later when we examine codependency.

_____
_____
_____
_____

3. Remember that the commitment of sickness and in health means being ready to be together through all events with minimal complaining and maximum encouragement.

Have a talk with your spouse or partner about each of your relationship needs when one of you is sick or otherwise down for the count. Make sure not to judge. Everyone is different on the road back to their own wellness. Common needs are rest, quiet, encouragement, touch, space, help with food or children, etc. If you're single, ask a close friend or family member to support you here, and make sure you try to find someone who has compassion in times of sickness. Write these needs down so you don't forget.

Sharon has had several serious illnesses beginning with cancer early in her marriage. God has healed her from all of them but they have taught her about relationships. She learned that her husband is phobic around hospital germs. Instead of being upset, she called on her secretary and neighbors many times to help bring things so he could come for the essentials of helping to bathe her and watch a program with her. We cannot expect our partners to be all things in all events. Focus on your partner's strengths. Be sensitive to each other's needs and do not fall victim to satan's lie of, *if you really loved me, you would. . .*

4. Reinstate self-care needs and set limits even though you're putting the other first.

I can't eat healthy because they don't, isn't going to cut it when you're both on high blood pressure and diabetes meds. Eat a balanced diet even if you sometimes cook grilled chicken for yourself and your partner wants lard fried in butter with a side of ranch. Your health is not contingent on theirs.

Similarly, *I can't save money because they spend it all,* will leave you both in the red. Decide in advance how and where to spend and save, and then invest some cash for the both of you that you can't touch, even if it's just a bit.

The body does not need the same attention as the mind but don't let your body atrophy completely. Do twenty crunches and squats a night even if your partner says you don't have time or money for the gym. Free weights, *YouTube* videos, and workout apps are inexpensive and easy to do at home.

What will you do each day to keep your personality thriving? Choose something in each area: physical self care, emotional self care, and most importantly, spiritual self care.

_____

_____

_____

_____

5. Redefine your gifts financially. Brainstorm what area each of you are best at. One of you may keep track of bargain hunting, and the other may be good at analyzing the budget. This helps to grow a nest egg for an emergency or if one of you gets sick or loses a job.

My friend Lisa didn't want to work outside of the home as a married spouse, but she got her college degree in case anything happened to her husband. He, a lawyer, died in his mid-fifties and because she had her teacher certificate, she went back to teach for another twenty years. In fact, she took my own daughter through kindergarten! She was even able to keep her beautiful home and help her children through college with a lot of penny pinching.

She taught my husband Wes and me the importance of having a trade or a backup plan even with a financially stable spouse. You never know what life is going to bring. It was GREAT advice!

Sharon had a similar occurrence, experiencing a divorce forty years ago. She received no alimony or child support because she did not want to alienate her children's father, especially in a time when divorces were rare. Relying on her teaching degree, she was able to support her family and to co-parent successfully.

What is your financial plan of action to support yourself in case of emergency? What gifts or trade skills can you rely upon? Think of more than one avenue in case certain doors close. If in a relationship, talk about this with your partner.

_____

_____

_____

_____

6. Recognize your own gifts and interests if you lose your marriage to a death or divorce you didn't want. God can give you back the time lost and redeem any hardships.

Again, Lisa made life meaningful even without her husband. Marriage is not the only way to a meaningful life. She poured her life into children as a teacher and into her friendships. To this day, in her early eighties, she still holds a Christmas party each year, since she's a gifted host.

Christa's dad wrote poetry and lamented about his missed wife after she died but he also had a female friend to share his writing with, he joined a book club, and he occasionally took a date to the Democrat club. Since he had retired from teaching with a good pension he regularly contributed to, he worked freely as a volunteer at a mental health outpatient facility and spent time each day with grandchildren.

Sometimes people leave, die, divorce, cheat, you name it. Can you survive this? Yes, you can. You were made well, and you can get through anything with God's help. If you stay close to Him, you will find your heart mending after time!

Don't be dependent on someone for every bit of survival. If you see this settling in, do something to challenge yourself to get out of that overly dependent mindset.

So having read these tips, are you ready to take the plunge? Gulp, right? Before we end this module, you should also know that a healthy marriage can be AMAZING!! That's why God created it and said it was good!

Bottom line? Marriage is an act of faith and you just don't know what you're going to get. Choose wisely, this is forever. But ultimately, if you trust your Creator's good leadership and you also do your part, you will win every time whether single, married, seeking, or simply dreaming of finding a long lost love!

Say a prayer to God for bringing you back to wellness, to balance, and to wisdom in your marriage. Make a specific plan to get the self care and to have the important conversations we outlined in this module before we explore the next section together.

When will you get self care this week? When will you have the important conversations outlined in this module with your partner and accountability partners?

_____

_____

_____

_____

MODULE 2: UNDERSTANDING GOD'S GOOD PLAN FOR YOUR BROKEN PIECES

After learning that Sharon has many degrees and accolades, as well as a thriving private practice, many people are surprised to learn that she has also had many struggles and spent years broken and ashamed because of them. Sharon has ADHD. As a child her work was messy, she broke things often and also struggled with learning disabilities and severe spatial difficulties.

As you know, our personality struggles do not disappear as adults. Sharon's struggles continued in her jobs as an adult and continue to this day. She recalls how God always meets her right in the midst of her struggles, and He always has.

In her earlier years, Sharon worked in a hospital for children with severe mental disorders. Though she was competent at the work, completing her paperwork was next to impossible because her handwriting was terrible. She was chided for it initially and felt shamed.

Instead of throwing in the towel, Sharon turned to God in prayer. Surprisingly, she found that the hospital administration was able to work with her struggles. They said that they could not read her notes, but because of her good work, they were going to let her use the doctor's transcription call-in line. What Satan tries to use as a weakness, God will turn to good. God will use your gifts in spite of your weaknesses.

Our point in this module is simple but profound. You don't have to camp out in your disability or your weakness, instead look at how God can use it. Be open to what He can do. Remember Philippians 4:13 here, *"I can do all things through Christ who gives me strength."* Don't remain a victim!

The life verse and mission statement God has given Sharon for her work as the founder of Family Care Counseling Center is found in Isaiah 61. See how God uses this passage as a promise to those of us who would cling to Him even through our hard times and imperfections and also be willing to grow. As you give your trials to God, He will give you double for your trouble. Learning disabilities gave Sharon the compassion for children. Obstacles become opportunities. She's chosen this passage as her mission statement for her practice.

"The Spirit of the Sovereign Lord is on me,
because the Lord has anointed me
to proclaim good news to the poor.
He has sent me to bind up the brokenhearted,
to proclaim freedom for the captives
and release from darkness for the prisoners,
to proclaim the year of the Lord's favor
and the day of vengeance of our God,
to comfort all who mourn,
and provide for those who grieve in Zion —
to bestow on them a crown of beauty
instead of ashes,
the oil of joy
instead of mourning,
and a garment of praise
instead of a spirit of despair.
They will be called oaks of righteousness,
a planting of the Lord
for the display of his splendor."

Take a moment to reflect on this passage. What do you see God saying to you through it?

_____
_____
_____
_____

What a beautiful reminder for us. Be encouraged, God will

use even your darkest days for His purposes if you give them to Him. He will literally turn your ashes and hardships into beauty one day. Make no mistakes, your trials will be your strengths to comfort others.

What imperfections and struggles do you want to give to God today? How long have you been holding onto them? A lifetime, like Sharon?

If you still don't think God is saying this about your struggles, visit 2nd Cor 12:9, 1 Peter 1:7 and James 1:5. God will use us despite our weaknesses and in many cases, all the more because of them so that He can be glorified. In other words, He comes through when we just aren't measuring up. Therefore, my self-esteem is not about me but how God views me.

Review the above verses and write down how God wants you to view your trials. If this is a sticking point for you, write the verses down and commit at least one of them to memory so you can keep it with you always! I (Christa) have 2nd Cor 12:9 memorized as it's something I needed so much in the past through times of discouragement that it was better to keep it inside of me at all times!

Our main point in this module is that instead of self esteem, God wants you to have God esteem. God esteem is a belief that He has given you certain gifts to use and when your weaknesses get in the way, He will make a way where there truly is no way. This using of your God-given gifts, and the infinite love from

23

Him, even despite your weaknesses is your God esteem.

Have you seen Him do this for you before? What is your response to this?

For example, If He chooses to raise me, Sharon, up as a leader or allows me to be a good grandmother, wife, teacher, in all of this, I am so happy to do it, so thankful, so honored. But if and when I have harder days or moments that are a little crazy making, this too I know, is part of life.

If you lean on God, you will find your weaknesses aren't so important anymore and that God will bring a team around you to sharpen you. When we opened our counseling centers (we each have a different practice) we prayed for a team of soldiers committed to the same mission we had, to heal the broken hearted. Surrender the impossible and God will provide.

What do you do to keep yourself as healthy as possible when you're going through stressful times? List your natural antidepressants, not necessarily the medical ones, though those are helpful to some. For example what gives you a lift? A walk on the beach, playing with the dog, calling a friend, listening to worship, watching a movie, buying someone's dinner. For some of us, a sure-fire way to get a lift is to do something for someone else. Bake a cake. Do an errand for someone. Buy them a gift. For another, it's an hour or two to relax with your spouse or on your own. For still another, a vigorous workout will snap them out of a bad mood the fastest.

Who are the people you can see God placing around you for your current journey? Who could be sought out a little more for this in your circle of influence? Make sure to choose positive and wise individuals who would not steal your joy, be jealous or cause temptations. Who are your chicken soup people? They are worth their weight in noodles. Identify them. Send them a note of gratitude. Nurture these people.

_____

_____

_____

_____

In addition to using our strengths and letting God have our weaknesses so He can make beauty from ashes, God also says we have the power to renew our minds and to take every single thought captive. Some of our other hallmark verses are Romans 12:2 and Romans 8:1, as well as Philippians 4:8. In these verses, God reminds us that not only are we not condemned for struggling, but that we can choose how to think, and we can choose how to act, even under duress. Take a moment to look up these short but profound verses and to write them down. We challenge you to memorize one of these as well!

_____

_____

_____

_____

_____

_____

_____

_____

So should you *never* think about the hard times or the difficult emotions? No, choose to face them, painful as they are, and then speak positive life-giving thoughts and promises of God back to them. God will use these to minister to others.

You can also make a gratitude list after you go through something difficult. At any rate, don't forget the step of processing your difficulties. Facing your problems and imperfections is indeed a necessary step to growth. Recognize what you've been stuck in or hurt by and offer it up to God. Only this can bring the changes you need and allow God's miracle to be seen in your life.

What are you grateful for? Wear the attitude of gratitude moment by moment and it will retrain your thinking. It takes twenty one days to build a habit and sixty two to keep it going strong. Set a phone reminder and keep it going even if you miss a day here or there!

_____

_____

_____

_____

When you do this, instead of a healthy self-esteem, you get a healthy God-esteem at the end of the day. There is a difference. See yourself the way God sees you. Man will always let you down, but God is the same today as He is forever. You realize that while your mate may not esteem you, God does. He made you and loves you just the way you are.

When Christ died for you, it was for past, present, and future sins. He does not hold you ransom, but instead paid that ransom price so you could walk in light and freedom, using your gifts as a trusting and healthy, beloved child of God.

Spend a moment thanking God for this incredible gift or talking to Him about this.

_____

_____

_____

_____

When you think the world may fall apart around you since you won't be the one "running the show" or your little corner of it anyway, it's both humbling and relieving to learn that God can and does consistently work in the lives of those you care about and in your own life when you surrender to Him.

God can use you at any age, twenty or eighty. Marvelously, He really still uses you, perhaps even more, to bless others in your seasons of pain. Again, remember 2nd Corinthians 12:9 as you consider this. *"But He said to me, "My grace is sufficient for you, for my power is made perfect in weakness. Therefore I will boast all the more gladly about my weaknesses, so that Christ's power may rest on me."*

Rewrite it here below so you can really remember just how real it is that God uses your weaknesses and turns them around.

_____

_____

_____

_____

You won't do life perfectly each time, you will still struggle, but our hope and belief is that we all continually embrace these truths of God. You will never be the same again and your family and ministry will be so much stronger. You will gain a healthy God-confidence, and you will use your gifts in a brave way like you've never done before. Your community influence will be stronger, because as a broken but beloved child of God, you're more relatable than someone who's perfect. People want to know you too are broken, and that there is hope for them in their brokenness.

To see others leaning on God in their brokenness is so motivating. So remember, on days or in seasons of struggle when you're not quite as put together, God still loves you every bit as much as He does on the good days. He loves you not because of what you do, but because of who you are, His child.

MODULE 3: RECLAIMING YOUR TRAUMA

I (Christa) remember completing a Minnie Mouse puzzle as a child only to find upon completion that two of the pieces to put together were missing. I still have the picture of me with a toothless grin holding the puzzle at certain angles so no one viewing it would be distracted by the gaping holes. My mother is the one who snapped the picture. I smiled widely and knew I had done my best. I also knew had her unconditional love. This kind of love seemed to come easily to her, surely because she knew brokenness very well having survived a mental health diagnosis when stigma was at its peak. I often hid those pieces from would-be critics who weren't quite as generous with their love. Isn't that what we do in relationships with those broken pieces sometimes? And neglect to mention them on social media?

Here I am, we say, *All perfectly polished and put together....Just don't look too closely*! And when we bond with others, the personal puzzle gets more complex. Now there are more pieces put together, ours and theirs, *and* more missing pieces.

Who have you hidden your true self from over the years? Media? Friends? Kids? Spouse?

Try as we may to pretend we're perfect and have it all together, those personality puzzles will never be fully complete unless we let God finish His masterpiece within us, as we mentioned in the last module. But sometimes these missing pieces have their root in a trauma we've experienced that we haven't been able to let go of yet.

Do you have a wound that you think is keeping you from God's best for you? What is it? What hurts you about your childhood? As Sharon wisely reminds us, unexamined pain will resurface and unresolved wounds drive our behavior.

_____

_____

_____

_____

Maybe your spouse has gone through a trauma and you're reading this with a bitter heart, painfully acknowledging that their pain started long before you even met them.

He always storms off just when I start to talk about my issues...

She nags me the minute I get home from work and even sends me texts while I'm there even though I do everything for her...

He always flirts with other women while we're out together...

She demands all of my attention even when I have very little to give...

What do you think your spouse or partner is facing in terms of trauma from their past?

_____

_____

_____

_____

I realize that as you consider your own unique trauma, along with your spouse or family, sometimes you'll find that it's not just the simplest things missing such as a night of board games, "I" language or a balanced budget. Sometimes it's *big* things, like knowing how to get deep enough to sit with others in the dark places, like knowing how to stay faithful maritally, like knowing how to stay away from an addiction, and knowing how to seek healthy forms of nurturing. If you find someone you're dating cannot bond, our advice is for you to break it off. Don't think you can fix them, you can't.

If you're already married, when you're tempted to blame your spouse for their shortcomings fully, will you stop to consider whether their past trauma or issues has informed their current situation before you rush for a divorce? What are *you* filling your hole in the soul with these days? Shopping, alcohol, volunteering to exhaustion, food, sex, etc.?

This is big with extramarital affairs. It's tempting to blame a spouse entirely for their affair. It certainly shouldn't be blamed on a loving, nurturing spouse who is close to perfect. But is anyone really that perfect? Perhaps that's why Jesus told the elders to step away from the woman who was caught in adultery and to look at their own sin in John 8:1-11. Often the past of someone who had an affair is quite complex. Perhaps they were in an unloving marriage where they were disrespected or unloved for years. Perhaps they felt on the edge of sanity because of it and especially because they hadn't invited God into their pain to heal the wounds. Maybe that's all they ever knew from their family history and they had no trust or had been abandoned.

If you're contemplating an affair, listen closely. Affairs are ALWAYS a mistake. They are fantasy and not real life, they avoid dealing with the problems directly, and they are wrapped up in sin and lies. This kind of relationship is *not* blessed. It may feel good in the moment, but be sure, Proverbs 2:16-22 reminds us not to fall for this. *"Wisdom will save you also from the adulterous woman, from the wayward woman with her seductive words, who has left the partner of her youth and ignored the covenant she made before God. Surely her house leads down to death and her paths to the spirits of the dead. None who go to her return or attain the paths of life."*

Have you ever dealt with an affair? Looking back, what were other factors besides sin that may have contributed to this pattern of relationship distress?

_____

_____

_____

_____

Trauma will never be a pleasant memory but often you get the sense you've worked through it, and it's time to let it go. Even though affairs are fun for a time, in the end they do not heal the wound but indeed sometimes add to it in various ways. *Have you worked through an affair, or major trauma issues for the most part, or do you feel there is some major work to be done in order to heal well?*

_____

_____

_____

_____

To be a pioneer and to forge a new path takes hard work, and sometimes mistakes are made along the way. Be open to understanding this, whether someone's struggling with an affair, people-pleasing others outside the family, being cold, being critical, being overly dependent, being suspicious, being neurotic, or their own form of struggle. There are so many ways we fail one another, and sometimes it's trauma based. We don't need to rush into a divorce or a quick fix. We need to take time to understand healthy individual and family patterns. Individuals need healthy self care practices in place of these struggles, in the spiritual, emotional and physical sense.

A helpful tool as you examine your own and your family's trauma is the *ACE Trauma Test*, which is free online at various sites, both electronically or as a self scoring test. A score of 10/10 means you have experienced a large amount of trauma, whereas a score of 0 means that in childhood you didn't experience any. Most adults are somewhere in the middle and still more trauma can be experienced in older years. This test can help you to understand those who have more trauma, such as a PTSD war veteran, or those who were heavily abused as children, may not be as well equipped in their emotional health toolkit of sorts. These individuals will almost certainly have a harder time negotiating emotions. It will lend compassion to your heart to take the place of the current seed of the bitterness you have carried towards this person. Take the test, and if your partner wants to, encourage but don't force them to take it as well.

Remember this, too: ACE scores don't tally the positive experiences in early life that can help build resilience and protect a child from the effects of trauma. Having a grandparent who loves you, a teacher who understands and believes in you, or a trusted friend you can confide in may mitigate the long-term effects of early trauma, psychologists say. *"There are people with high ACE scores who do remarkably well,"* says Jack Shonkoff, a pediatrician and director of the Center on the Developing Child at Harvard University. *Resilience,* he says, *builds throughout life, and close relationships are key. Recent research also suggests that for adults, "trauma informed" therapy — which can center on art, yoga or mindfulness training — can help."*

So as you consider your own past and your partner's past and work to reclaim your trauma, will you be like the wise elders in John 8:1-11, who were planning to stone a woman caught in the very act of adultery? After Jesus spoke to them and released the woman from shame, the elders were the very first to drop their stones of blame as they realized that brokenness is complex and part of all humanity.

So will you be like them and more importantly like Him? Will you offer your family healing and support with your understanding and love during their moments of weakness? And, like Jesus with the woman in John 8, will you boldly and lovingly call them out of darkness to a higher ground? Will you challenge them to rise to a better standard while holding a loving and safe space for them? Take a moment to pray about and to plan for this.

_____

_____

_____

_____

Knowing each of your individual stories, how can you uniquely use your gifts that have strengthened or emerged from this traumatic experience? James 1:5 reminds us that our trials bring perseverance and character and 1 Peter 5:10 says, "And the God of all grace, who called you to His eternal glory in Christ, after you have suffered a little while, will Himself restore you and make you strong, firm and steadfast."

_____

_____

_____

_____

I have noticed God always uses every piece of my story to help someone, even and especially my traumatic pieces. It's an amazing feeling to realize that God has not let that pain and suffering be in vain but has used my life to teach someone else while He heals me also. That's a win-win and a promise we find in both Genesis 50:20 and Romans 8:28. Take a moment to read these amazing and redeeming verses. Respond to God with gratitude and any insights you have received after seeing these verses.

_____

_____

_____

_____

The journey may also be quite a long road with several reroutes. But, Sharon reminds us and our loved ones, *"Reclaim your trauma but do not camp out there. Process the wounds so you can come out of your comfort and into your calling."* We can become comfortable staying stuck in our misery. I know that does not sound logical, but the negative becomes the familiar, and it is hard to break into a new way of thinking, even if it is better for us.

While that calling may not be full of ease and comfort, God will make a way where there seems to be no way.

God provides like streams in the desert, as He lately reminded a client and me while praying (Isaiah 43:9). God had a sense of humor choosing me for ministry. I later learned that God deliberately uses wounded people to do his work as he uses our pain for HIS glory. Experience is what gives us our credentials. My disabilities became my credentials. What we have been through in life can be used to help others if we look to God to guide us. God doesn't call the equipped, He equips the called.

An unexamined wound will resurface in all of our relationships. These wounds will drive our behavior and cause us to fill that pain with an idol like shopping, alcohol, porn, food, etc. The hurt will exert control over our life and drive our behavior. Bring those secrets out of darkness and into the light. God will use the hurt for His glory and for your blessing.

As you work on your relationship, if you recognize that one or both of you have trauma that's contributing to your distress, use the following tips and tools to keep you on track:

Stop to reflect on what happened when you or your significant other lose ground emotionally. Did one of you give the other cues that you were getting flooded with emotion and the other still barreled over? Did you bring up a difficult topic that is deeply painful for one of you? Offer grace if so. Taking short breaks, following it with a fun activity, or scheduling it for a later time can help. Writing things to one another via messaging means can help, too.

Does one of you cry at the drop of a hat? If so, is there something that was never grieved? An unresolved death or a childhood that needs to be attended to or prayed over with compassion, even briefly? Who do you trust to share your story with? It is important to find someone you trust to help you process your feelings and to validate the pain. Sharon has worked hard at cultivating a few dear friends she can talk to when she gets stuck in unresolved hurt as have I.

Does one of you say "I'm leaving," but not say, "and I'll be back soon....." Or "This conversation is over," but not talk about when it can continue? Don't leave your spouse in the lurch just because you're feeling badly. Let them know you're returning and that you love them. Don't throw around the word 'divorce' as you're hurting and healing and growing together. Your partner will never open up safely if they think you've got one foot out the door all the time. Make a checklist of your own codependency issues so you can realize what you're still struggling with personally instead of attacking others when they cannot be fully Jesus to you.

Has one of you had an affair? If so, make sure you get some outside support to help you process it. Find someone who has your marriage and family in strongest mind as they help you both to recover and to wisely forge ahead.

Maybe as you stop to consider that it's not just your spouse who's broken but you also, you will extend more compassion and grace. The spirit of offense is common in wounded people. The enemy wants you to be offended. Then he has the power in your actions, not God. The enemy wants to keep you from shining your light and helping to set people free.

Either way, as you open yourself up to a life with God and spend time with Him healing, you'll extend more forgiveness and love to others. You'll be better able to use your gifts. You'll be surprised at how much your spouse or family may love and help you as you continue to grow comfortably together to an old age. Every relationship has an ebb and flow and good seasons and bad seasons. Be careful to patiently push through the bad and not to catastrophize the temporarily uneasy season. Like the weather, the sun will come out again, spring is around the corner.

Remember this, God died for us on the cross so we have grace here and now. Like Christa's mom, He lets us smile through our broken pieces. But He also wants to heal us. He knows that as we lean on Him, those broken pieces are no longer a hindrance. In fact, He was broken for us so that our weaknesses may be of no consequences to the end result of His work in us. (Isaiah 53:5, 2nd Cor 12:9) The more you love, the more love you get back from God, both here in some ways and also in Heaven. Celebrate that about God's love over you, toothy gaps, missing puzzle pieces and all! :)

MODULE 4: NAVIGATING MALE AND FEMALE BRAIN DIFFERENCES

Seriously? You don't think I can throw the ball as far as you? *"Nope,"* my big brother said.

My brother was sadly correct in his bold assertion to me (Christa) that day and I'm sure more than a bit disappointed with having three sisters and no brothers to work on his baseball throw with him. Still, he ventured to teach his younger sisters many sports, including basketball, wrestling and boxing, only to find out that while we all loved athletics, we sisters often wanted to play with our dolls and do one another's hair and makeup. This continued over the years as well. I wanted to coach not only my friends but also my dolls through their relationship woes.

To help my brother bear his lonely cross a little, I was Pac-man one Halloween and cheered on with him vividly at all of the Pay-per-view wrestling matches he ordered. Most of this I ended up discarding for decidedly more of my own interests, which included a mix of activities, some coed and some traditionally more feminine, such as makeup and braiding hair. Sometimes men and women are just different, and those varying differences can leave us puzzled and asking questions like, *"If men are from Mars, where does the female brain reside?"* This kind of thinking often leaves frustrated males and females up at night, wondering and even agonizing about all these differences.

Is this OK that in this module, Sharon and I are being that honest about the roles we step into sometimes, even comfortably? Stereotypical of me to say? Perhaps, but we notice the roles we lean towards as males and females are quite natural and the research tends to concur. What exactly does the research say about our brain differences and commonalities? What does it mean for us in our current relationships?

Well first of all, it's both fun and conversational for us to talk about a "right brain" versus a "left brain." It's been found that some of us do indeed prefer more "left-brained" activities such as logical puzzles and focused analytics whereas other individuals have a more natural proclivity toward "right brained" creativity and intuitive features.

However, the stereotypes of these fun brain personality conversations do not have their foundation in brain science, but more belong in the personality theory of temperaments we'll be studying in Modules 9 and 10. To use them in this format is perfectly fine if we're doing it for the purposes of the assessment of and the 'meaning making' narrative of our personalities. *Have you ever bought into the right and left brain theory? If so, which one do you tend to lean towards?*

_____

_____

_____

_____

If we want to talk actual brain differences, we need to move from the lighter personality assessment "right and left brain" conversation. This is because just as the inner workings of a computer are interconnected, everything in our brain is so intricately tied together that it's just too difficult to say one or the other activity is truly "right" or "left brained." This is not the case when it comes to the male and the female brain.

First, God makes a distinction as we note in the Creation story, that He has created us male and female in Genesis 5:2. He distinctly tells us this, and we can all easily notice a woman's body is made to hold life and other bodily differences and functions as well.

As we move into scientific processes, we can also find actual differences between the male and female brain development and the way information and feelings are processed. For those feeling really upset right now, perhaps because they defy stereotypes and we all do to some degree, there will always be overlap and anomalies. But normatively, there are some main differences.

What differences do you you see inherently in men and women, if any?

_____

_____

_____

_____

Have you ever been hurt or challenged because of your gender? If so, how? Do you think you're holding back anything because of it?

_____

_____

_____

_____

In <u>general</u>, males have some tendencies we can notice in nature:

- They are often more physical and show affection by wrestling with each other.
- They are often taller.
- They are often more aggressive and less emotionally sensitive.
- Their spatial processing/ability allows them to rotate objects more easily/geometrics/physics.
- They are usually more into physical features when seeking a partner for reproduction purposes.
- They are logical and detailed and have of a more focused type of processing, fix-it nature.

Females also have some tendencies in no particular order:

- They are often better at multitasking and have the ability to switch tasks.
- They more often have depression.
- They are more likely to pick a secure financial and/or older and

taller mate.
- They are more likely to pick a man based on his storytelling abilities, whereas men are less likely to care about that. Females often like to process their feelings and examine a narrative.
- They are more likely to process emotionally and have a longer memory for emotional distress.
- They usually have a larger hippocampus/memory center.

If you think all of this may be because of stereotypes, think again. Most people actually tend to lean even more into their "stereotyped roles" in egalitarian cultures such as Sweden where you find less a less pushy or defined stereotyped culture. What do these gender preferences or leanings mean for those of us in relationships?

Whether we meet those criteria personally or not, I believe it helps us to empathize and to understand. Often times, our male counterparts simply don't get it or can't relate to some of the things we do as females and vice versa. That doesn't make any of us wrong, it just makes us all different from one another. That's an important and sometimes forgotten distinction. We want to remind you that finding someone *exactly* like you of the opposite gender ultimately may do you more harm than good. You will likely instead find lasting chemistry with someone who has some commonalities but also complements you and is somewhat different from you. Those in relationships must know this to be true.

I know this is true for my family. I remember zeroing in on my husband as a future mate due to his opposite gifting. That lacking spatial relations quality that earned me my first and only D made me clamor for someone to balance the equation (sorry, math joke!). I respected Wes for it, and I finally paid attention to his persistent pursuit of a date since prior to that he seemed like a typical jock, which according to our list about what females want, really doesn't make the cut.

As much as your spouse's unique quirks may irritate you,

when you find that person who balances your equation, you begin to realize that together with you and your strengths, this person offers your family a life more fully in line with what they deserve, a still imperfect but much more complete package of human capacity at its finest, working in tandem for the good of all.

MODULE 5: UNDERSTANDING HOW LOVE LANGUAGES & BIRTH ORDER INFLUENCE US

My family loves to laugh about an old home movie where I'm a toddler chasing a ball. One of my older siblings keeps snatching it from me and once again, the ball is always just a bit farther ahead. As a baby, I didn't seem to catch on that I would never catch up and so the "funny" cycle went on! I'm grinning as I write that because I know it's par for the course for a youngest child. Some of that kind of sibling toughening helps you to be just that - tough.

What is your spot in your birth order? Middle, oldest, youngest, adoptive, step, middle? List how you think that role may have shaped you for better and for worse along the way in your relationship(s)?

_____

_____

_____

_____

In my instance, in a world where we're decreasingly allowed to comment on actual winners of a race and where everyone gets the same medal, seeing the video is almost refreshing. Let nature takes its course, right? Thankfully, there was a lot of love and protection from those older siblings as well, times when riding the bus was a little easier knowing there were three older siblings to cushion the blows of new life in the big wide world for a little while.

So do these kinds of birth order beginnings follow us into our adult lives, or do things balance out enough to just leave us alone once we enter the world of society and all that the pecking order implies? What happens out there on the school bus when the siblings have up and graduated school on you?

Both current compelling research and info going all the way back to early psychologist Alfred Adler tells us birth order indeed follows us not only into early adulthood but also into our marriages and relationships with our own children.

However, and take great care to notice this, your *perception* about how your birth order influences you is what influences you, *not* the actual birth order. For instance, if you were born first, and you've been told firstborns are smart leaders, you'll approach a test with more confidence.

In effect, just as we stressed the importance of controlling your thought life in Module 2, taking your thoughts captive and believing the best about your gifts has more to do with actual success than does birth order. Still, a family's leanings and preferences along with their projection of who you are in the family ranking order does affect most of us to some degree.

How do you think your perceived birth order influenced you and still influences you?

Finding yourself in this birth order conversation can add to awareness and lead to a better quality life. And please, feel free to share your story with us as well!

I, Christa, married a firstborn, and as the story goes, firstborns often have some key traits: leadership, responsibility, organization, detail and helpfulness. This sounds a lot like the Enneagram 1 as you will read in Module 10. By no coincidence, most of our presidents and a great majority of our astronauts have been firstborns. Many times their parents critiqued them for their small flaws. *Only a 95 percent on the test? What happened to the other 5 percent? Next time, right?* There's no one else to distract these idealistic, nervous, and well-meaning parents in the way of other children to manage. Thus, all of their hopes and dreams (and retirement plans) may fall as a burden into the lap of a oldest or only child.

These children often learned to feel very much like a human experience of guinea pig shaping. They carry all of their parents' own disappointments and failures on their shoulders as well as those of themselves, their younger siblings, and in the case of presidents, sometimes the world.

My own eldest child surely can relate. I know when I hear a weary sigh, it's time for me to examine whether I've put too much pressure on her yet again. I remind her (and my husband) that I love them for who they are, not their accomplishments or perfection, since no one is perfect.

If you're an oldest (or only, who typically follows the pattern), this can follow you right into your marriage and family as well. You could be dictatorial or perfectionistic, halting progress and minimizing grace on your family and even yourself if you're not careful. A huge tip for growth is this: High standards of excellence are important. Given with grace and sandwiched by genuine compliments, you'll be heard, and your (usually very good) ideas will be received with gratitude.

Sharon is the oldest of three and had to pave the way for the next siblings, too. The mantra at her house was, *"You are the oldest, you should know better."* To this day, she is a rule follower and is super responsible. She also feels her parents lightened up their discipline with her younger siblings.

Who do you know that's an oldest child in your family? Do they follow this particular pattern? Whether it's you or a loved one, how can this person find encouragement?

_____

_____

_____

_____

Middle borns often feel pressure to please everyone around them. Because they're sandwiched between at least two others, they can usually also wind up being quite competitive to gain attention. They have the unusual skill of being able to blend in like a chameleon quite well wherever they go. They quickly learn the fine art of appealing to their parents, their oldest siblings and their younger ones too with acute social skills, often making this child better at socializing than others, not to mention diplomacy in conflict. This can concur with Enneagram types 3, 6 or 9 quite often.

The biggest worry that often falls into the lap of a middle child, or perhaps sorrow is an even more appropriate term, is feeling that they aren't noticed. Locked in between a whiny baby and an oldest who's already on the path of meeting all of the parental dreams, a missed middle child doesn't feel like they have as many foreseeable options in terms of getting their needs heard.

Sometimes they handle that by becoming the loudest but more often their social merging offers them the advantage of being peacemakers in their society and excellent social companions in both marriage and work. Sharon's middle grandchild is very quiet and if not careful, is likely to be forgotten. Her son is careful to give this child her own sports of cheerleading and gymnastics. She gets along so well with everyone. The oldest in this family makes her needs known and the baby is, well, the baby, but the middle two go along with most everything.

Only children have similar traits as the oldest but need much more alone time. They usually have larger vocabularies as they relate to adults very well. As they get older the only child likes to have time more by themselves and may find it hard to share as their have never had this predicament before. This need for privacy comes from not having siblings barging into their personal space. They tend to score higher on tests and go to college more than the other birth ordered children. They can be bound by personal to-do lists and have never had to go by other people's rules. Getting the only child into sports and play groups is important for social skills building that they naturally lack. On the flipside, they can entertain themselves without the need for socialization as much as children with siblings. Only children may find themselves feeling entitled and perfectionistic, unable to handle disappointment.

If you love a middle born, make sure you look into their eyes and make them feel heard. Make sure you encourage them to pursue their interests instead of always having to go along with everyone else. My (Christa's) middle born feels this often, so I make it a point to look directly into her eyes and make her feel special on a daily basis. I try to work very intentionally to reverse the roles of what is unfortunately a very real tendency with most parents, including myself, of sometimes missing out on this fabulous person who's so eager to please those around her.

If you're a middle born yourself, remember, it isn't only others who are special and need to be heard, you too need to exercise your own gifts. You can voice your opinions even if others disagree, and even if your opinions don't always win or you lose the race, remember, you're still loved, uniquely gifted, and valuable.

Who do you know that's a middle child in your family? Do they follow this particular pattern? Whether it's you or a loved one, how can this person find encouragement?

_____

_____
_____

_____

Last born children often follow a pattern of being coddled or doted on and don't alway feel the confidence of the older siblings (and how can they if they never can get to that ball!? :) They can also charm a parent with their lowly position. I can remember so many times crying into my mom's blouse, even though sometimes the tears were feigned for extra cuddles when I was the one who had been naughty. I felt like the misunderstood underdog who was too young to go trick-or-treating, had the earliest curfew, and generally "couldn't do anything."

However, don't coddle a last born too much or they won't thrive and you'll have a spoiled brat on your hands. I can still remember my older siblings' comments that were biting at the time but helpful in shaping me (*"You cry everyday, when are you going to grow up?"* And *"Mom, don't spoil her, you're giving into her every whim."*) These phrases made me take pause in my tears. I can still remember stopping to consider whether this was true when I heard these shocking remarks. Did mom coddle me?

Years later, those experiences of tough siblings helped me to both win and lose tennis matches with courage, to run hard on the track team with endurance even though I wasn't the best, to be a more gracious wife who learned she isn't always going to get her way, and to be a parent with perseverance since we all know that's not an easy job!

My own son is a last born and when he did Vacation Bible School this summer, his older sisters and I were unintentionally doing everything for him, down to the zipping up on his backpack. My wise oldest daughter (of course, my oldest!) who helped in another kindergarten class, woke us up when she saw others his age, *"Mom, these kindergarteners are doing so many things themselves!"*

Little Jack didn't know what hit him when I firmly made him do things for himself the next morning. He learned to zip that day for sure. If you love a last born, make sure you help to raise them up with dignity, a can-do attitude, and plenty of chores and work, even if they try to charm you out of it. If you're married to one, enjoy the fun and laughter they bring, but don't be surprised if you have to remind them when playtime is over!

Who do you know that's a youngest child in your family? Do they follow this particular pattern? Whether it's you or a loved one, how can this person find encouragement?

_____

_____

_____

_____

Remember this above all: Your perception of how you are means more than the actual birth order. If there are tendencies you don't like about how you were raised as a first, last, middle, only, step, adoptive or another form of guardianship, *you have the power to make those changes in your life, despite the shaping.* You are not an animal but a human with choices. The Bible clearly says that we are made in the image of God to do wonderful things in Genesis 1:27.

It won't always be easy to leave the old mannerisms behind, but taking the best of them with you ahead, while letting go of the worst of them will bring you both successes and lasting joys!

Your Love Language

Our perceived birth order influences but doesn't always affect our idea of love languages. For instance, an older child who did all those chores and babysitting may love acts of service as a love language. Middle borns may love quality time and last borns those special words of affirmation, the baby talk we often hear going on between couples! But this is not always the case so it's extremely important that every individual wanting a healthy marriage regularly check in with your spouse or partner about their favorite ways of being loved.

I read a story written by a well-known pastor years ago, and it's stuck with me ever since as a prime example for discussing love languages. That is probably due to the fact that I've since heard it similarly stated many times over from various couples over the years. At any rate, this pastor thought giving his wife the same "clearance" flowers he found on his way home each week would be just the ticket for making his young bride feel loved.

Several sad exchanges later, he finally figured it out. This attempt was certainly not being interpreted by his wife as loving. Especially not this style of cheap giving. Love costs something, doesn't it? Not only does it cost, but it's also a verb, an action which varies day to day and season to season, a fluid language, if you will. The concept of love languages isn't a staunch, one-size-fits-all that's the same for everyone each moment.

Remind your partner of your favorite love language. What do you think is your significant others'? Don't forget to ask them if they aren't completing this with you! Mark their answer into your calendar as a regular challenge so you can try to love them in their favorite way one small way each day.

Although perhaps you may immediately think of one thing or another, such as when your spouse does kind and loving acts of service, or when they tell you something great you've been longing to hear, sometimes your love language shifts. For instance, when you experience grief due to a job or a physical loss, you don't need your spouse to simply do the dishes. You may need a comforting touch, a kind word or a small gift. If you're one to get overwhelmed, you may actually just want the help with chores. People are unique in their quirks and preferences, and yet we do have some similarities.

I (Christa) have worked with many couples who almost lost their marriage over one spouse not realizing how important emotional connection was for the other. This happens more than you realize. Many women feel their men, for instance, only want sex, and women resent them for this. Men do tend to love physical touch but most men want their spouse to fully enjoy their sexual experience or (as they've told us) they would just pleasure themselves. It's *connection* they're seeking with their wives; it's their natural way of showing love. However, it's also important that they recognize their wives' favorite ways of being loved. When we go out on a date night, my husband knows my usual expectation is for quality time and his is for physical touch. Each of us has our own love language and we don't pretend otherwise, nor is it cookie cutter or legalistic, since needs vary over days and seasons.

When we understand the science of love, it makes life much more pleasurable. When the days are long and arduous, as they are at times, it's wonderful to have someone who has done their homework and "gets" you, isn't it?

But when one spouse feels like the other one isn't loving them or hearing them, it's tempting to think you're not loved at all. There are severe cases like this, which we will cover as we talk about codependency in the upcoming modules. There are also times when otherwise healthy spouses are just plain in the dark about how to reach one another in love.

This is where the concept of love languages helps people along. Gary Chapman talks about five specifically; Willard Harley in *"His Needs, Her Needs,"* adds a few others. Sharon and I both think that there are an endless variety, so don't be small-minded as you try to consider your favorite ways for feeling loved.

Sharon has clients who tell stories of loving their feet rubbed, others who love to be remembered with thoughtful gifts for birthdays, holidays, or just an "I was at the store thinking about you gift" (Come to think of it, who doesn't like that once in a while?!). Some need to be encouraged in their jobs the most or in their marathon training, some need space and some breathing room with gentle tones. Do not expect your spouse to read your mind nor you theirs, ask them and tell them.

Don't think you have to be like other couples either. We've never met two alike, and that keeps our jobs very interesting. Just come into it with an open mind and also an open mind to your spouse changing from time to time in these matters. For the free online traditional love language quiz (it ranks them in listed order very neatly), take it at www.5lovelanguages.com. Don't count every little thing your spouse does after that for better and for worse by love languages. Remember your own self care as you make your needs clear, but don't control. This brings us to codependency next.

MODULE 6: LETTING GO OF CODEPENDENCY IN RELATIONSHIPS

From the time we were four, Kayla and I did everything together - fun, mayhem, and creating unforgettable neighborhood lore still laughed and groaned about frequently in reminiscence. Suffice it to say, we were #twinning it with the best of them before hashtags were the thing. If Kayla succeeded, I was happy, if I succeeded, she was happy. If she succeeded with another best friend, I was...

Ticked.

Some of you reading are nodding internally about your own insecurity capacities or seasons where you wanted to be someone's #1.

What were some of your codependency triggers growing up?

_____

_____

_____

_____

In this module, we're talking about the important concept of codependency in relationships, and now we want to especially highlight why it is has NO place in your marriage. As you all know, the new little girl's "bestie" when she becomes an adult, is ideally her significant other. Many times, however, we feel as though our spouse can fill in every single need and heart gap, that as Saint Augustine said long ago, only God can fill. Whenever we put our complete dependency and happiness onto another person it's called codependency.

Here's a rule of thumb as you consider codependency. Men and women really do need one another for survival but they also both need God for thriving. There's no getting around the fact that women and men are inextricably tied up together in destiny. As much as a woman may say she doesn't need men and a man say he doesn't need women, so far as we can tell, we really do need one another and science has not yet proved otherwise.

But what if the other person doesn't love us as well as we feel we need to be loved? What if we feel like we can't survive without them? If we could put words to a codependent unconscious thought pattern, it would be, "I depend on someone else for my security and happiness more than I do my own ability to create it and more than I rely on God." And since you're going to inevitably find disappointment at some time in another flawed human, it's also a relationship killer. Humankind will always let you down in some way but God will not.

I still remember the day Kayla told me she wasn't going to be under my thumb anymore. I had no choice but to release her and by this brave stance (hers) and the release of control (mine), our friendship survived. We are still good friends today! At the time, I was initially sad, truly. I had thought I was a good leader and it seemed like the one person this youngest sibling could lead. It was like the idea of projection, when the boss yells at the employee, who yells at their spouse, who yells at their dog. Kayla was my place to vent and let off steam. That cycle "works" for survival but doesn't take her health or mine into account. No one is thriving under that system. When we use systems like this, it's typically an unhealthy defense mechanism called projection, pushing our own feelings of pain and helplessness onto another person, the new victim in the never ending cycle.

Instead of following this pattern, healthier individuals learn to stop projecting their pain onto others and take everything upwards to God. He's our Maker after all, and nothing is too hard for Him, as we mentioned in Module 2. Trying to control people in your life will not earn you the love and trust you hope to hold. Instead, trust is earned by loving and respecting that person and yourself as well.

Even though now I know how to avoid codependency like

the plague, it still gets me every now and then since I'm still in the process of sanctification, becoming more like Christ. I'm pretty sure that without even realizing it, some of you are stuck there all the time, in this early childhood development stance that's no longer productive, simply from habit and hurt.

If you're not sure whether you're dealing with codependency in your relationship, here are a few telltale signs:

Signs of Codependency

- You often force your spouse into things they don't want to do, or you agree with your spouse even when on the inside you have a bad feeling about it.
- You often rationalize your own bad habits or theirs without confronting them even if they're dangerous.
- You always put your spouse above everyone even when they're being inconsiderate of everyone else.
- You and your spouse don't respect one another as human beings or offer grace.
- Your self-esteem is at an all-time low.
- You resent your spouse for hanging out with others, even when the others are good people.

Here's how codependency differs from the healthy interdependence of a relationship:

- Codependency says, "What's good for each of us personally doesn't matter so long as we keep peace." Interdependence says "We both matter. I'll make sure we find a solution that brings us both peace even if it takes some time."
- Codependency says, "I have to say yes to this person or they'll leave me." - and - "I have to force them to do what I want." Interdependence says, "I can trust God. Still, I won't say or do anything that compromises my values and dignity."
- Codependency says, "I know abuse isn't what the kids and I deserve, but if I rock this boat, it will be worse." It may also say, "I must force someone to love me." Interdependence says, "My

relationship is in the pits. I'm going to make sure we seek help. I'll need to set some boundaries into place to protect us all."

Do you think you are acting codependently in your relationship(s) now? How so? Try not to beat yourself up, just name the situation(s) and follow our tips below:

_____

_____

_____

_____

Tips for Healing From Codependency

- Start prioritizing your self-care. Don't wait for your spouse to jump on the bandwagon.
- If and when your spouse is abusive in language, take a step back from the conversation. Confront control, speaking the truth in love, like Kayla did with me.
- Do a Bible study on the Bible app under the topic of boundaries. What does God say about keeping your relationships healthy? The Bible app has a great one called, "Boundaries 101" that can help you! Bonus, the Bible app has many great studies if you need a distraction and more info, it's always free! :)
- Get your thoughts out in writing or with a wise mentor so he or she can help you to stand strong when it's something you firmly believe in or to make graceful acquiescence as needed. Soon that internal gauge of your own will help you to do this on your own.
- Remember your spouse or family member has their own issues and perhaps even some trauma. If they're willing to stoop to ridiculing you, it isn't even about you, it's their own rooted hurts they're still acting on. This says more about them than you. Don't take it on as a truth about yourself. You know you have God's grace, and you can glory in your weakness knowing there is where God's power rests on you most vividly (2nd Cor 12:9 again).
- If it's a dangerous situation, flee. You were given a fight-or-flight

instinct for this very reason. After you're out of immediate danger, talk to wise counsel about what to do next.

Remember, as you take these tips, and as you release your terrified grip on another person for validating your existence, give yourself grace. You are at this codependent spot for a reason and that reason was probably something difficult you experienced when you didn't have the tools to get out of it. Here are also a couple of great verses for emerging from codependency, *"If God is for us, who can be against us?"* and *"What can man say about me?"* (Romans 8:31 and Hebrews 13:6). *Greater* by MercyMe is a great song to give you courage during a codependent season. These reminders have not only helped me through difficult moments when I wanted full control, they have blessed me as God Himself has time and again helped give me more than I could ever ask or imagine as He promises in Ephesians 3:20-21.

You can also find a hobby or gifting that you deeply enjoy that your spouse does not have to do with you. For instance if you're a teacher, perhaps it means learning a new skill, helping a special child, or working on making your classroom activities vibrant. If you're an animal lover, enjoy your own pets with extra love and care or foster another pet. Whatever you do, don't start telling yourself it's OK to find another person of the opposite gender to enjoy emotionally or physically on a one-to-one basis. This is an affair in the making and yup, you're still being a codependent.

One more thing, if you're realizing now that you're actively struggling with codependency, take a few moments to think of three things about yourself that you love. It could be your kind or sparkling eyes, your generous smile, or your bold countenance. Even when others don't see your worth, God always does. God sees you as His masterpiece. Ephesians 2:10 reminds us of this. *"For we are God's masterpiece. He has created us anew in Christ Jesus, so we can do the good things he planned for us long ago."*

Take a moment to respond to God for loving you this much. Do you feel a renewed echo of hope in your life? What does it spur you on to do? How does it make you feel?

_____

_____

_____

_____

MODULE 7: ADDING FUN TO YOUR RELATIONSHIP
+ 50 GREAT DATES

Even though the science and processing of personality and relationship building is so essential, we'd be completely remiss if we forgot to mention the simple joys that God also intends for couples. So if you really want to take your relationship to the next level, this module will help you to keep a healthy dose of fun in your lives together!

Sharon and I don't just have fun and easy lives of enjoyment 24/7 in our relationships. We have both worked so hard on our marriages, sometimes even carrying it for our spouses when they were going through difficult times personally. They've also carried us through difficult times. You'll find that if you stay married long enough, you'll see that it has many ups and downs where one spouse carries the other. This is literally stated in the Bible, in Ecclesiastes 4:10, *"If either of them falls down, one can help the other up. But pity anyone who falls and has no one to help them up."*

What's a season in your relationship where one of you has held the other up?

_____

_____

_____

_____

There are seasons of plenty and goodness and seasons of trials and tribulations in a healthy marriage, make no mistake. Sharon, having had cancer and I (Christa) losing my parents at a young age were not easy things for our young husbands, nor have their hardships and weaknesses been easy for us to bear. Don't let the enemy trick you into thinking trials have to hurt you. Trials, as the Bible reminds us, make us stronger, as we are reminded in James 1:3-5, *"...You know that the testing of your faith produces perseverance. Let perseverance finish its work so that you may be mature and complete, not lacking anything. If any of you lacks wisdom, you should ask God, who gives generously to all without finding fault, and it will be given to you."*

Trials *only* take you down if you give up on God's good plan for your life and also give up on refueling as needed. If you're trying to take a weekly date night or day, or even a few shorter at-home dates a week, you can keep the fun going no matter what season you're in.

I, Christa, remember when my mother had a stroke. I was a twenty-one year old bride, and mom was a supportive, Christian mentor and giver of unconditional love. She was a listener and friend to my young husband and me, who were finally out of our teen years and starting to appreciate her. Almost overnight, we got the call from my father that she was reduced to the level of a two-year-old. That would last for the next twelve years of her life until she went home to Heaven.

During the early part of this time period, our date nights were the only times in the week I could just let down my guard and stop focusing for just a little while that I had, in effect, lost my mother. As I was a wilder teen who did the typical individuating, I was very blessed that the last few years had been changing me, helping me to rely on God's strength to get me through. We visited her almost nightly that first year of marriage, offering company to my bereaved father and trying to work out her new system of care. Dating my kind but naturally bewildered husband consistently through that season helped to keep me young and fun as I should have been at that age. I can't tell you how important it is to keep doing these things to avoid caregiver fatigue, even when the world tells you you have no time or that you "should" be in constant work mode, mourning mode, or service mode.

If you have any doubt about God's desire for pleasure in your marriage, listen to what He says about simply enjoying your marriage, in Ecclesiastes 9:9. *"Enjoy life with the woman whom you love all the days of your fleeting life which He has given to you under the sun; for this is your reward in life and in your toil in which you have labored under the sun."*

What is God saying about marriage here in this verse?

_____

_____

_____

_____

As we grow, God is telling us that we need to enjoy our marriages, that amidst the hard work of the day, these sweet stolen moments with a spouse are not only OK but also blessed.

So whether you're a newlywed, a retired couple with tons of opportunities for fun, or a struggling middle-aged couple with few supports or opportunities to get out, this is the spot in the workbook where we help you to find that fun again or for the very first time. We've suggested fifty dates for you, knowing everyone is different and has varied interests. Trade who gets to pick so it isn't just always the same spouse deciding the fun. If you're the planner by nature in your relationship, don't let that frustrate you into not planning since your spouse never does. That's your gift, enjoy it and bless your family! Many of the options we give here are at home, are free, and are easy to do after the children go to bed if you can't afford a sitter. We gave a lot of tips for everyone and encourage you to add your own as well!

Whether you're having a formal date or not, we recommend connecting on a no-stress level about ten hours a week. This could be breakfasts or lunches together as well as one date night a week or include watching your favorite show together nightly.

Try to have variety and consistency, even if you have to schedule it on the calendar. You are worth it and so is your relationship. Don't talk much, if at all, about stressful topics on these short dates. With about one hundred and twenty waking hours in the week, try to save other times in your week for the "coupon" conversations you need to have about laundry, stress, bills, and dishes! These date times do not have to be out of the box or completely extraordinary, they just need to have relaxing qualities for both of you, at least to some degree.

Fifty Great Date Night Ideas

1. Make homemade pizza together with each of your favorite toppings or create ice cream sundaes.

2. Work out together with some stretching and holding one another's feet or another form of touch. It will feel good and your munchies together afterwards won't induce as much guilt.

3. Snack together. Challenge yourself to choose creative or just plain delicious foods to eat together from what's at home if the budget is tight or enjoy some special take-in. If you cook, try a new recipe to make something yummy to share, and keep an old standby in reserve if it's a flop.

4. Go for a drive in the car if the kids are old enough to be at home or if not, snap them into car seats and give them something to do while the two of you coast, think, listen to music and chat together at least part of the time.

5. Put the kids to bed a little early after tiring them out as best as you can. Play a grown up board game not involving breaking any ice or a familiar barrel of monkeys.

6. Have a carpet picnic dinner with candles or a few fake or real flowers for ambiance.

7. Wives, do your makeup or hair just like you would if you were going out for a nice night on the town. Guys, take a shower and shave though you're just at home. Little gestures

impress and bless.

8. Clean the house, dim the lights, and put away the piles and work that will be waiting for you tomorrow.

9. Put some tunes on the radio. In fact, put something on your spouse loves. I normally wouldn't choose country music but when I remember to, I (Christa) sometimes play my husband's favorite country music and he plays Jack Johnson to relax me. If he's around, it sets a nice tone.

10. Community parks are great places to just take an easy stroll together. Sharing a meal out, and then going for a walk, can keep your steps light and your budget light as well.

11. Set an hour of conversation with no electronics or phones and just talk like the old days when you were dating.

12. I (Sharon) ask couples to get creative on their dates, asking questions of each other such as, *If you had an extra one thousand dollars or even a hundred, what would you spend it on? What did you like about each other when you met? What career would you like if money were no object?*

13. Visit free festivals, of which Florida has one every week.

14. Pick strawberries or local fruits together! Farmers Market morning dates can be fun, too!

15. Visit a MLB baseball game or a practice for spring training or during Fall or Winter, support your local high school football and basketball teams by going to a game.

16. If you're local, window shop in Village of the Arts or the St. Armand's or Pine Avenue shops. Mall walking is fun too.

17. Our beaches are the best in the world. Sunsets are usually gorgeous and the weather usually cools off by that time of

day! A sunrise jog or walking date works too!

18. Think coffee. A date can be for a coffee or cocoa or tea, simple and comforting.

19. If you're local to Southwest Florida, Robinson Preserve and Emerson Point Preserve are beautiful, as is the Venice Bike Trail.

20. Many venues have dancing and you can join your local Moose, Elks or Eagles as well. Don't go dancing without one another on most or all occasions; dancing can be very seductive and is meant to be enjoyed with your love!

21. A picnic with bird watching or kite flying is exhilarating and something most couples don't take the time to do.

22. Thrift store shopping for your favorite collection or puzzle is fun. Not into puzzles? Try a game of cards, Skip Bo or UNO.

23. Love animals? We have the top rated small zoo in United States in Tampa, the Lowry Park Zoo. We also have the Big Cat Habitat, Jungle Gardens, the pretty butterfly garden at Selby Botanical Gardens, and Mote Marine. Look up your local deals for your own local dates.

24. Mutual massage is awesome and cheap if you just practice on one another. Intimacy of any kind is a fun finish to most dates for a couple where one or both spouses have a high need for sexual connection.

25. Make your favorite dessert together after your kids go to bed if your budget is tight or you're not that hungry.

26. Wash and detail each others cars for an extra special "acts of service" date. Play fun music while you clean.

27. Rollerblade, bike, rent Segways, kayak or even rent a golf cart

at the beach.

28. Plan a staycation at a local 5 star hotel or beach villa. There are also many one tank trips that have a complete change of scenery in Florida or your local state. Anyone who has been to Ocala or Mt. Dora will appreciate the change from the beach.

29. Have neighbors over for a barbecue.

30. Train for a 5K walk or run together or even a triathlon.

31. Take an art or photography class together. You can do this on the Internet now also for free on YouTube or for a minimal fee.

32. Have kids spend the night away and plan a surprise gourmet meal and special time for the two of you at home.

33. Relive your first date.

34. Go ice skating. We have several rinks even in tropical Florida.

35. For your spouse's birthday, have a fun scavenger hunt around your town and have the people you get clues from in on it. They may even have a treat at the place for them!

36. Make up a new game that the two of you share with others! Creativity and putting your brain together for new projects can keep things exhilarating after the newness of a relationship has worn off!

37. Trading Netflix night is fun. You trade picking a movie back and forth, week by week, so you don't have to spend too much time disagreeing about which one to get!

38. Make donation boxes and have a night to start throwing in old trinkets for a good cause. Drop them off on your way out to eat.

39. Visit the drive in movie for cinema and cuddles!

40. Read a book to each other or let Alexa read it to you together.

41. Try an ethnic restaurant together.

42. Make a list of ten things you are grateful for and compare notes.

43. Put on a favorite show and sit together. The point is, be touching so you can enjoy connection even while you watch.

44. Create a scavenger hunt just around the house!

45. Hang out at a bookstore and find books you think your partner would love in five minutes or less! Peruse travel or art books, have coffee, and dream.

46. Have friends over for a mystery dinner game. Christa and her husband Wes write games for their company, Supper Sleuths, and have had a ball playing these games with many other couples over the years.

47. Go bowling together.

48. Do a late night cruising date. Stop for fast food and listen to tunes. You can even do this one in your jammies!

49. Celebrate holidays together on dates *near* the actual holiday. Another idea is to get off work a bit early and have a late lunch. Don't skimp on your love but don't waste two hours in line either!

50. Visit an archery or target range together!

As you can see, there are so many fun ways you can connect with one another, plus you can even add things neither of us added here! The most important thing is, have fun! Marriage is hard work, don't sacrifice your playtime. God has given you free time together not just for working on stressful family issues but also for fun. Remember Ecclesiastes 9:9 when you struggle with this. He has given your spouse to you for not only support and partnership in the hard work, but also for some planned and spontaneous fun and for joy together!

Which of these are you wanting to try first? What number appealed to you first? Make a creative and concrete plan to get these dates in regularly.

_____

_____

_____

_____

MODULE 8: NAVIGATING UNIQUE SITUATIONAL CHALLENGES

As much as we love talking about personality types and styles, relationships have a wide variety of issues. In this module, we talk about the unique issues couples face. Some of these issues will apply to you, while others will not. We encourage you to read this short module in full so you can have a basic understanding of how to get through the experiences we talk about here. You'll be better equipped with difficult situations both now and down the road.

In order to find out what family patterns are found in the lives of our clients, we often do a family map, called a genogram. This map helps the couple to see family patterns and to take a good hard look at these family of origin issues. These generational maps help the counselor or coach understand how, even if you don't have various presenting problems yourself, having relatives with major weaknesses and disorders can affect the family system. There are also of course, strengths to be gleaned. Many couples have never looked at their family history and lineage of addictions and mental disorders.

What family difficulties and disorders are in your family system?

_____

_____

_____

_____

What family strengths are in your family system?

_____

_____

_____

_____

What family difficulties are in your partner's family system?

_____

_____

_____

_____

What family strengths are in your partner's family system?

_____

_____

_____

_____

When I (Sharon) was in grad school, we spent time evaluating not only our clients family system, but ourselves through this lens. There are many positive stories in my family. Since Otis is my last name, it was good for me to learn that the name Otis is affiliated with the elevator and the steam shovel. My nephews have both invented something significant for two major corporations and have been very successful with their inventions. My brother is a pastor, and as we consider our spiritual line, I hope and believe we have broken some generational bondage for good.

When I continued to explore our family history, I learned that there is raging alcoholism and mental illness throughout the genealogy as well. My parents were married for sixty-three years, which was a credit and a strength my family. However, if my mom and dad had only talked about all four grandparents dying of alcohol-related disease and great grandma's secret illness, we would have been more aware of the long-term issues plaguing our families. Sometimes we judge those in our families or our spouse's families as being weak, immature, selfish, or needy. It takes more effort but is worth it to be loving if we accept our family members when we see that they are now, and were, hurt children.

As I reflect on my family tree at large, I can see now how alcohol was also used to cope with depression. There are even still family secrets that I tried to get information about, but my parents died with only a few clues spoken aloud.

Take a good look and see if there are signs of depression, alcoholism, gambling, pornography, autism, ADHD, anxiety or any other disorders in your family story that may explain some of your parents behavior or even your own. Back in the late 50's there was not much information known about ADHD and that really influenced my (Sharon's) childhood. I was spanked at school and then spanked at home for being distracted, for not completing work, for having a messy desk, for being unorganized and impulsive, etc. What helped me was learning about it in grad school so I could help channel my weakness to help my son and other children with learning disabilities.

My husband has Attention Deficit Disorder, so he too has focus problems, just without the hyperactive features. *"How do two ADHD people get married?"* I asked my psychiatrist friend, Dr John. Dr. John said, *"Look at your Facebook page. You two have so much fun together."* We both realize that having fun together is a strength, but behind closed doors we have to encourage each other to make deadlines and to stay organized. I give my husband lots of grace and he gives me grace also.

I also have learning disabilities and poor visual spacial problems as I mentioned earlier. When I pour a glass of milk, part of it goes out of the cup. As a child, I would get slapped for this but my husband just grasps the washcloth and mops it up. We try to understand each other's weaknesses and not make a big deal as we both have faults. Having ADHD is not an excuse to stay stuck. I have various degrees and certifications, and keep my home in order, but it takes more effort than for the average person. I have to be intentional every day. I am not sequential so I make a mess and have to go back and be sure everything goes back where it belongs. It's important that as these family stories help you gain insight about deficits, that you focus on the good and accept the imperfect in yourself and in one another.

As you look at disorders in the family, you may see

perfectionism, depression, many addictions, obsessive compulsive disorder or other anxiety-provoking issues. Learn what you can about your family, but be kind to yourself and to anyone with whom you are in a relationship as you learn about their issues. Sometimes anxiety or depression are the result of abuse as a child, growing up with an addicted and untrustworthy parent, being abandoned, or being the sibling of someone who had special needs. Take time to learn why you and your partner act the way you do. Hurt people hurt people. Many books are written on the effect of broken family systems and how to break the cycle with your family.

We do want to set aside one caveat about tolerance. Abuse is not to be accepted under any circumstance. It's not to be tolerated any more than Hitler's methods of eugenics and abuse were to be accepted.

Personal boundaries are crucial to a healthy relationship. Yes, the person doing the abuse is broken, probably had a bad childhood, and probably isn't very happy. Treating another person in an abusive manner is never the answer, and we are all adults who know truth. Please make sure you get help immediately if you are degrading others or being degraded with physical or emotional violence. There are doctors, therapists, and other caring professionals in your church or workplace that can help you. Don't stop until you find the right individuals to help you and your family find a way out of this. You are ALL worth it.

MODULE 9: THE ORIGINAL TYPOLOGY: DISCOVERING YOUR TEMPERAMENT

What's all the hype about type? Some of you have been waiting for these later modules where we get to talk about your personality types. But where did this originate? God differentiates our gifts in the Bible in various spots: Psalm 139, His hands formed you, Romans 9:20, He purposed you, Jeremiah 1:15, He set you apart and has a plan for you. Most vividly, 1st Corinthians 12:1-11, was mentioned in an earlier chapter. In this section of the Bible, we see the way God distributes gifts. It's so neat that God literally and uniquely creates each temperament, type, and gift. Read this important passage of the Bible to see this for yourself.

"Now about the gifts of the Spirit, brothers and sisters, I do not want you to be uninformed...There are different kinds of gifts, but the same Spirit distributes them. There are different kinds of service, but the same Lord. There are different kinds of working, but in all of them and in everyone it is the same God at work...To one there is given through the Spirit a message of wisdom, to another a message of knowledge by means of the same Spirit, to another faith by the same Spirit, to another gifts of healing by that one Spirit, to another miraculous powers, to another prophecy, to another distinguishing between spirits, to another speaking in different kinds of tongues, and to still another the interpretation of tongues. All these are the work of one and the same Spirit, and he distributes them to each one, just as he determines." Corinthians 12: 1-2

As you took a moment to read what God says about the gifts He gives us here, which one or ones do you think you have? How can you use these gifts in your home, church, and/or vocation?

_____

_____

_____

_____

We also know that personality study was happening as early as

400 BC, when the philosopher Hippocrates was a physician. He studied his patients' various personalities with great care and thought. With his extremely limited phlebotomy options, he thought that an excess of bodily fluids or humors is what caused the four main personality types. To this day, we use the labels he gave us for the main types, sanguine, melancholic, phlegmatic, and choleric. Hippocrates's theory of blood "types," if you will, is no longer popular, although one could argue we now do recognize different blood types. We also appreciate and use his basic and quite helpful depictions of personality to this day. Others that followed him, such as Adler, Erich Fromm, Arno and Tim LaHaye have continued to use the temperament theory to explain people at their basic levels.

Our temperament is placed within us by God while we are in our mother's womb and remains with us throughout our lives. How we choose to express our temperament is affected by our upbringing, our environment, our education or training, and the work of the Holy Spirit in our lives. Temperament determines how we interact with our environment and the people around us. People can elect behavior that is a mask to hide their true temperament. Every person has different temperament needs with strengths and weaknesses.

The Sanguine Temperament

Both ancient and modern theorists recognize that some people have a sanguine temperament that is playful and loving. These individuals thrive on daily adventures with other people and children, such as in a classroom teaching or being part of a project, with lots of positivity, and enthusiasm. Sanguines have a great energy to them and when understood, validated, and loved, these individuals can thrive in a wonderful way. It's important that if you are a sanguine personality type, you realize that when others don't match your speed or style, it doesn't mean they don't love you, they're just different and not many can match that energy. You reduce stress by doing things with people, and your spouse may reduce stress by being alone. Have empathy for the different types. Also, sanguines often marry someone they can help because they have so much overflowing love to share and love their relationships so much. Unfortunately, sometimes this sanguine individual's personality is largely built on people pleasing so that they're actually very unlikely to realize when someone is taking advantage of them or using them. *Guard your heart*, Proverbs 4:23.

It is so important to realize when others abuse your loving nature and steal your joy. A great book for sanguine types to read and to incorporate is the book, *Boundaries*, by Cloud and Townsend. You will find when you set limits with others and take some time to personally replenish daily, you're actually quite good at taking care of both yourself and others to some degree. No spouse will ever meet your complete need for love and affection so it is important to talk to God. You also begin to ultimately realize that others must eventually learn to grow and take care of themselves and that you are worthy even without their constant affection and attention.

Study the verse John 15:2, as you begin to release relationship slavery and find common ground, self respect, and continued loving others with preference. Then you'll know who to keep in your life, and who you may need better boundaries with, or in rare cases, whom with which you need to stop relating. This verse says, *"He cuts off every branch in me that bears no fruit, while every branch that does bear fruit he prunes[a] so that it will be even more fruitful."*

Are you a sanguine, or a super sanguine, like Sharon? How can you make sure you take good care of yourself as you care for others? What tools can you take with you for your growth? How can you honor the sanguines in your life?

_____

_____

_____

_____

If you're a melancholy individual, you enjoy order, beauty, depth of thought and feeling. You are easily swayed by a poetic thought, a mood piece of music, or a philosophical bent, and once you feel strongly about something, it's difficult to move you in another direction. This means if you're in a brooding mood, it's quite hard to get you out of it. If you're in a joyful spirit, it can be enjoyed to the full. You experience these swings and those around you must know this about you if they're going to make this last the long haul.

In other words, a melancholy person without much self-growth can be critical when upset and a delight beyond comparison when happy. Don't let them scare you about yourself. Your own personal growth comes in realizing that for a healthy bond in marriage, you must still love and respect others even when your mood is down. You must still work, you mustn't hurt yourself or others, and you must learn that these deep emotions can be processed healthily. Melancholies are thinkers so they need to pay attention to their thinking. We don't think positively naturally so a melancholy must teach themselves to look at a cup half full, not half empty. If they are rejected, they can get very angry. Know your perfectionism and critical side and master it. This temperament is very creative and can see things others cannot see like an engineer, architect, landscaper or artist. Historically, artists are called temperamental for a reason.

Don't think going into a sullen tizzy for days on end is going to produce an immediately patient mate, or that when you come out of it, revived and raring to go, others will be immediately forgiving. Instead, tell your spouse when your mood has taken a turn for the worse, and then allow yourself to indulge it for only 30 minute to 2 hours. Play some music, write in a journal, have a good cry, but don't turn it on others. Instead, remember that feelings mustn't be your guide. Also celebrate that you do have the gift of being able to help others who have a dark moment since you get it. When you come back to the light, allow your spouse a little time and space to adjust, apologizing if you were critical or otherwise negative during that time. Your spouse is cherished in a deeper way than most can imagine ever being cherished. You shine brighter than even a sanguine when you peep out and enjoy life with a true child-like glimmer.

Are you a melancholy individual? If so, what tools can you take with you for your growth? How can you help people to understand your temperament? How can you honor the melancholies in your life?

_____

_____

_____

_____

The Choleric Temperament

If you're a choleric type, you're used to being in charge. You feel refreshed and most vibrant when you're in the lead and others can follow your bold and brave example. It's great to revel in and to enjoy this feature of leadership that comes so naturally to you. It's also crucial to remember that you need breaks from being in charge, especially in marriage. Marriages with a choleric partner need to have plenty of give and take or your spouse will feel like their opinion doesn't matter, and that you always have a better way of doing things.

Though cholerics lead in work-based environments, try working on expressing a softer side at home, embracing feelings even though they don't come naturally to you, and enjoying trusting a mate who loves you for more than just your savvy and achievements. Let them know you hear and love them and their ideas too, and mark off some time with your significant other intentionally in your busy planner if it doesn't come naturally!

Cholerics usually marry Sanguines but remember Sharon's phrase, *"Opposites attract but marriages attack."* The very things you like about your partner are the very things that drive you crazy. What did Sharon like about Dennis? He was laid back and easy going. What drives her crazy? He's laid back and easy going. What did Dennis like about Sharon? He liked her vim and vigor and her super responsibility. What drives him crazy? You got it.

Are you a choleric individual? Do not be like the bullfrog in a hurricane. They puff themselves up to appear larger but that coping mechanism is useless. What tools can you take with you for your growth? How can you use your temperament to thrive? How can you honor the cholerics in your life? Be sure to ask your partner what is important to them.

_____

_____

_____

_____

The Phlegmatic Temperament

If you're a phlegmatic, you're a peaceful individual who enjoys bringing quiet relaxation to the world. You don't always share your emotions as readily because you have such empathy about how others are thinking and feeling. This makes you especially diplomatic and what's more, excellent in marriage as someone who can really empathize with your partner so much more than others who may get stuck in opinions or goals. Phlegmatics are easygoing and often really do not care what movie you watch or activity you do because they want you to be happy. It is important if you are married to a phlegmatic that you go to movies you know they will also like, even if it takes patience to ask again.

As a phlegmatic, don't let others pull you around when you do have a clear sense of right direction. One of the ways you can protect yourself is by making sure when anger rises up because you haven't been heard or valued, that you address it with empathy and care. But do address the issue. Don't let your anger get the best of you in these moments. Be respectful of others as well as kind, but also be firm in your positioning. Only then will your partner be more likely to make sure you're heard and that sometimes *your* best ideas are put forward. Avoid sarcasm as well. Phlegmatics will bite to put people off when stressed, and directly addressing issues is a better approach.

Are you a phlegmatic individual? If so, what tools can you take with you for your growth? How can you make sure you are heard and getting your goals accomplished? How can you honor the phlegmatics in your life?

_____

_____

_____

_____

The Supine Temperament

A supine individual is a combination of sanguine and melancholy in many ways. This temperament was added a bit later by Drs. Richard and Phyllis Arno in 1983. Supines feel emotions strongly like a melancholy, but they also have enormous amounts of loving care to give like a sanguine. The problem they most often struggle with is that they don't share those feelings readily. Supines expect you to read their mind and get mad when you do not. Many partners don't understand how much they're actually loved by their servant-leader supine counterpart.

If you're a supine and married or hoping for a marriage, make sure you schedule a time each day to show your mate how much you love them. Ask for their "love language" and then respond to it. When you get moody, tell your spouse you need some extra reassurance if they can offer it. It's important that you find several places to get your high needs met and not rely on just them for it. People are not aware that supines present cool and walled off but they desire love and affection. Often their need for affection is never met, because they do not express that need since they truly believe in serving others first. Supines can take short breaks, but they suffer anxiety if away from people too long.

Are you a supine individual? If so, what tools can you take with you for your growth? How can you help people to understand your temperament? How can you honor the supines in your life?

_____

_____

_____

_____

Feel free to circle the characteristics and find which most resemble you and how you relate to the world.

Sanguine Temperament
Loves people
Loves children
Loves animals
Sensitive
Impulsive
Flits from task to task and doesn't always finish.
Lots of friends
Talkative
Undisciplined
Emotional
Extrovert

Melancholy Temperament
Creative
Intelligent thinker
Sensitive
Offended Introvert
Loyal
Moody
Perfectionist
Idealist

Choleric Temperament

Bossy/Leader
Selective Introvert
Practical
Goal oriented
Bold
Brash
Results-based

Phlegmatic Temperament
Calm
Sarcastic
Stubborn
Easy going
Gives in
Detailed
Slower-Paced
Relaxed

Supine Temperament
Appears cool but is really warm
Does not express their preference
Mostly a thinker
Combines melancholy and sanguine traits
Caring
Efficient
Servant Leader

Are You an Introvert or Extrovert?

Notice some of the personality types we've talked about and will talk about have introversion or extroversion as traits. This simply means you either derive energy from being on your own after a short or long time with people (depending on your degree of introversion), or that you prefer being with others most of the time to gain energy, meaning you're an extrovert. Introverts reduce their stress by being by themselves, and extroverts reduce their stress by being around people.

If this temperament viewpoint doesn't suit you, there's more to come but wait. Before you write off this temperament system, remember, this goes back thousands of years and has held merit consistently. You can take a great test version of it here, which offers fun charts and graphs. www.temperamentquiz.com

MODULE 10: FINDING YOUR ENNEAGRAM PERSONALITY TYPE

Can I get your digit?

You mean my digits, right?

No, your digit! As in on the Enneagram.

Oh my gosh, you're obviously a 7 goofing around so much. As if!

And you're obviously a 4, taking everything so seriously.

But seriously, what are you?

I'll tell you if you tell me first....

In our practices, it's been so very interesting to use various personality tests with clients over the years, such as the ones we're sharing here as well as so many others. Before I was a coach, when I (Christa) was an LLP psychologist in Michigan, I was trained to use the TAT, MMPI-2, and the MBTI, the FIRO-B as well as the 16PF, the California Personality Inventory, the intelligence tests, the WISC and the WAIS, and a variety of ADHD and depression tools. Whew, that's quite a list and the help I was able to give from all of the tests was minimal. Sharon and I have both used DISC and Spiritual Inventories, John Gottman's marriage tools, and Sharon has used the Hippocrates Temperament Test, the Arno Profile Temperament Test, as well as the PIAT, Bricklin and Slosson, to name a few.

What personality tests have you taken? Which ones have helped you with any lasting changes? What are you still wondering?

_____

_____

_____

Out of all of these tests we've given, none of the them have created quite the social buzz of the Temperament test and the Enneagram, and for good reason. We have enjoyed the healthy awareness that comes from reviewing and implementing the recommendations from these test results time and again ourselves, in our own marriages, and with our clients, friends, and family.

Though it is just getting big in social media in the past few years, the Enneagram has been widely studied by Christian spiritual mentors from all walks on life as well as therapists and even skeptics for decades. Many have chimed in with its validity and found common ground. Over time, scholars and laypersons alike have brought collective knowledge to study this simple and yet profound personality test. Although many generations were part of the development of this tool, in part it may have its origin in the church and even revolve around the seven deadly sins mentioned in the Bible at the core. At any rate, the many eyes modifying and shaping it over time have honed it into a helpful tool.

Perhaps this is because the Enneagram typing system not only types the personality, but also attempts to get down to the very core soul wounds that each of us carry around. It certainly doesn't replace the wisdom of the Bible or reduce the validity of scientifically validated measures. What the Enneagram does do is identify both our gifts as well as our weaknesses, as well as tells us how we behave in health, in moderate health, and in despair. It also offers us many tangible ideas for growth. If you've never taken the Enneagram test, you're in for a treat. We include the varying types and the struggles and strengths of each of them right here in this module.

If you're curious of our types, Sharon is an energized, extroverted and giving 2 with a 3 achiever wing and Christa is a creative and fun-loving 7 who goes to focused 5 as she writes and is introverted when she's not sharing that 7 joy. If you want to take the test formally, there are some great short and free versions of the test out there. The Enneagram Institute also has a longer (forty or so) minute version of it available for a nominal fee online at www.EnneagamInstitute.com. At the time of printing, you can also find a reputable version of the test at this address for free and even get tips sent to you by a coach at the following web address: https://www.yourenneagramcoach.com/p/yecassessment

We have also included a watercolor Enneagram chart done for us on the next page by the talented Amanda Dodson from Dodson Designs. As you look at the chart or discover your type here in this book, here's a hint at finding it. One of these numbers 1-9 on the wheel and in our descriptions should look as though someone has opened up your mail and read it, the fan mail and the gossip alike! Look at the wheel for a general clue and read our summary of each type to see if you were right.

If you relate to more than one type, don't be discouraged. You should be able to relate to all of them on some level. If we were perfect like God, we would have all of the strengths of each. Since we're individually gifted and most of us have particular strengths versus *every* strength, one of the types is detailed enough to be our main area of gifting. After all, we were each born with gifts and there is still much variety between each type since every person is a unique individual. If you've taken the test before, you may know your number already. At any rate, use this final module as a jumping off point for more awesome growth in your growth and relationships!

How to Use The Enneagram Chart

Find your core traits in bold on the Enneagram chart/wheel on page 89. For instance, if your main strengths are being orderly and industrious (a good worker), you're probably a Type 1. The bold words are some of your main strengths if you're a Type 1. The printed words just below it are a few of your core areas of struggle. Just below that, we find out which of the triads you're in for your quick limbic system or knee-jerk response to stress. As it

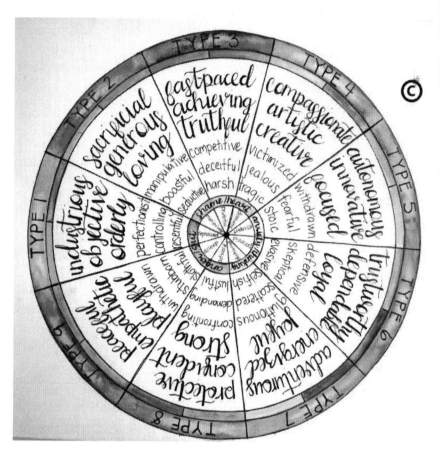

turns out, as an organized Type 1, you're in the "anger/body" triad, meaning you experience stress most quickly and naturally via anger in your body. However, if you look at the Type 1 by sliding even further into the middle you will see that even your anger type is specific. A 1 experiences anger as resentment, and that is often bubbling below the surface. Pretty neat chart, huh?

There's even one more special feature of this chart if you're using the online or Kindle version of the chart in color. We've shared some of the other dominant features each type experiences just under their number. So the Type 1 is turquoise but if you look just below the Type 1 border, you'll see two more colors directly below it, yellow on the left and magenta/pink on the right (Note

88

to black and white readers: You can find these other features by looking at your basic type on Enneagram Institute online for free otherwise where they will show you the "stress" and "health" arrows for each type). The left side indicates more strengths for Type 1, which for a Type 1 are also the strengths of the Type 7. A healthy 1 also can look at the bold labels of adventurous, energized and joyful descriptions of 7 since those also apply to a Type 1 in health. However, the magenta/pink leads a Type 1 to also realize they share the struggles (or printed traits) of a Type 4 in stress, which are a victimized, tragic, and jealous mindset. Again, on Enneagram Institute's website, if you type in, "Enneagram Type 1" you will see their chart points to 7 and 4 as well.

In addition to these tools, there is one final piece to the pie. While you connect best with one type, you also scored closely to two other types, so it's also nice to know which of those two sides you tend to learn towards. If you're a 2, for instance, you almost scored as a 1 or a 3 since those are the numbers just around you. You will be helped by noticing which of those "wings" you lean on more. So if you're a 2 with a 1 "wing," not only are you a helper, but you also love organization, justice, and can be good at seeing details objectively. Many times someone leans heavily on one of their "wings," and when they learn to balance both sides of it, they have even more great tools at their disposal. The more positive traits we exude, the better!

For instance, my (Christa) husband Wes is a 1. He leaned more heavily on his "2 wing" for a long time, meaning not only is he a neat and orderly 1, but he's also an oldest child who tends toward the role of a helper. That's great, but when he leans on his "9 wing" he is more peaceful and relaxed. Sometimes he intentionally leans that way even though it doesn't come naturally, just sinking into his "dad chair" and watching fun shows and eating snacks with family instead of the typical hustle and bustle of a 1 with a 2 wing. This is helpful for me as a 7 who loves to have lots of fun and introverted recovery time, even though I still like being social sometimes.

Sharon, as a 2 obviously loves helping, and she leans on her 3 wing a lot, which is her achievement side. She is a helper naturally and never happier than when she's helping someone through a problem, whether it's a family member, client, child, or animal. She also enjoys working and achieving, and that really makes her happy. However, she leans on her 1 wing as she manages her schedule and bills for her and her husband. This is very helpful to them.

So as you take a look, we want you to get excited about your best features. Use them to the best of your abilities and get to know them as your superpowers no longer kept secret. Use them in hard times and good times alike, and recognize others do not share your exact gifting, so try to give them grace also. Remember there's a reason only God fully understands why they developed differently from you.

Along with the best features, every personality also has a darker or shadow side. If you're married, you and your spouse can vouch for the fact that your beloved personalities also have ways of grating on each others' nerves at the most inconvenient of times. Perhaps you can be quite a bear when you get in a mood! This difficult side seems to offer us a character-building opportunity, right? Again, one of these types should fit you quite well and be a growth tool for you to try to work on as you celebrate your gifts.

Now that you've viewed the chart with your type, it's time to look at your personality a little bit closer. Take some time to find your number in the following pages and read more about it in depth. You can also feel free to find the type of your spouse or family member, but let them self-identify so they don't feel overwhelmed by labels.

Type 1

Alice is a 1, and after surgery, she organized every cupboard in the house, labeling it neatly. The bringing of order to her life added meaning and seemed to make her heal faster also.

1's are often called "The Reformers" since they bring helpful changes and order to the world. A healthy 1 brings their gift of organization, energy, and goodness to everyone they can reach. They create organized environmental systems for us to function within. At their best, they add order and strive for excellence, not perfection and impossible standards. They struggle with being controlling, resentful and judgmental at their worst since they are often overworked and insecure.

1's not only spend their time serving others, but also adding beauty and compassion to the world through various art forms and helping fields, embracing their own and others' flaws as something God, not them, made in His perfect timing. They realize true perfection will not be granted until Heaven. They take joy in just being a part of it at all here with this healthy mindset.

1's are why we have clean hospitals, why our books are edited, and why our road systems are organized and detailed. They are engineers, accountants, and quality reviewers, helping us to be strong morally and physically. This is because Type 1's are good at finding and correcting errors in the world. The cleansing and bringing order actually brings them a peace like nothing else, so they don't usually mind doing it.

1's have a deep God-given drive that allows them to work longer and harder than everyone else, or at least it feels so. 1's must recognize everyone has not been gifted with the same gifts, energy or stamina they have. They do well to recognize these are gifts given to them from God that are not promised for even one more day. Then they can enjoy rather than resent that they can do so much and also intentionally take time to view others' gifts that may complement theirs, such as the gift of relaxation that the 9 brings.

A 1 does best to take time for relaxing after the hard work is done. Most 1's have had a lot of responsibility since they were children whether self-inflicted or by choice. Some may say 1's can be critical, but at the end of the day, a secret about 1's is that they're more critical of themselves than anyone else. A verse they do well to reflect on is found in Romans 8:1, *"There is therefore now no condemnation for those who are in Christ Jesus. For the law of the Spirit of life has set you free in Christ Jesus from the law of sin and death."* At their best, 1's can be visionary, artistic and fun, in addition to being organized, efficient, moral and logical.

If you are a 1, what are the gifts and superpowers you can be proud of? What tips will you take with you from this knowledge of self?

_____

_____

_____

_____

Type 2

Carrie is a type 2, a doting mom of five and a creative and fun teacher. When I found out if she was a 2, I asked if she liked the humane society and she laughed, "I'm the president of my chapter."

2's bring their gift of helping others and adding love to the world. They also bring the gifts of compassion and beauty. 2's are passionate about protecting the helpless such as children and animals and fiercely show their care to others with their long bursts of energy.

In health they allow others to receive their help and gifts with freedom instead of forcing their gifts on them and then expecting them to reciprocate in kind. 2's are such loyal spouses, sometimes even to an abusive partner, so accountability and therapy is good for a 2! They can be manipulative, seductive, and controlling at their worst such as when they feel unloved, insecure and ashamed. If you are a 2, we would say you're amazing interpersonally, a befriender and a helper, an advocate for many.

2's love to be part of a team process, not necessarily always leading, but happy if they're proudly working on a project they believe in. Their creativity and fun lends itself to most others warming up to them quite quickly, as well as trusting them deeply with just about everything. They trust their feelings will be cared for and privately kept. 2's care deeply and will help a friend in need just about anytime.

If a 2 puts too much value on what others think of them, they can look with pride on their accomplishments and expect others to revere them for their achievements since they view themselves through what others say about their worth. If a 2 is unhealthy, their inner mantra is, *I'm OK if you're OK with who I am and if social media thinks I'm a champion.* It can lead to unhealthy but ultimately empty pride that doesn't fulfill. It can lead them into manipulating others into loving them back when the other person may not want as close a relationship as they want. This can push away the very people who wanted to be close to them because of their amazing gifts. Find friends who generally reciprocate too, versus only people to rescue or manipulate. Other 2's are out there!

2's also have another special gift. They are gifted with their intuitions about what would be helpful to others in the neighborhood, at church, or to friends and extended family. The spouse of a well-meaning 2 lacking boundaries may sometimes say, *"You're signing us up for too much. We can't help the whole world!"* or *"I can't meet all your needs."*

As they develop healthy boundaries, 2's will also take time for self-care, but it's very difficult for them to say no, so sometimes they forget about the self care piece of loving, the part where Jesus says to love yourself well also. 2's are loved, too, and worthy of taking some much needed time for themselves in the same way they love others so readily. This verse, Psalms 139:13-14 is important to remember here. *"For you formed my inward parts; you knitted me together in my mother's womb. I praise you, for I am fearfully and wonderfully made. Wonderful are your works; my soul knows it very well."*

If you are a 2, what are the gifts and superpowers you can be proud of? What tips will you take with you from this knowledge of self?

_____

_____

_____

Type 3

When her mother died, Callie was the first to order the funeral arrangements and did not immediately process her pain. She made sure her eulogy speech was written well and that everyone had proper attire and behaviors for the service. Only a week later when it was all over did she allow herself a little personal time to grieve.

3's bring their gift of achieving and bold truth-speaking to others in the world. Their workplace savvy gets every job or task done, including complex processes. A type 3 finds worth through leading others in a work setting, performing well, often writing stellar reports and loving trends and data. In health, they start to trust God instead of referring to achievements or an "idealized" mate to meet all of their needs. They must find non-addictive ways of calming themselves from their frenetic achieving. A healthy 3 does well to occasionally move from the hunt and chase of corporate thinking to a softer volunteer organization or family time to use their gifts. This still stimulates their strong and fast-paced, competitive minds but in a more well-rounded and caring fashion.

At their worst, 3's cut corners and can be unaware of their own feelings or disbelieve others really love them at their core, since many 3's lost connection with a parent as a child for one reason or another. They scramble to get needs met in addictive ways or through flashing their achievements. In this mad scramble for approval and love, 3's can come across as brash, harsh and deceitful. Some 3's say they felt most prized for their achievements as a child or didn't get much affection, so they now express emotions very reticently and feel most secure when they are achieving or showing off.

3's love being in the spotlight and are very popular and quite witty! Many type 3's do not experience many feelings besides anger and joy regularly, since they aren't as willing to read their own deeply buried and vulnerable emotions with the same ability with which they can perceive others' feelings.

Since 3's tend to pick up on things pretty easily, they often take the lead, even if it means cutting corners on unnecessary parts. Sometimes 3's wear deceit as a defense mechanism and shadow side, but that's when they feel unsafe with someone. Often thought of as chameleons, 3's may wear the mask of whoever they want to connect with, to project connection, and to win love.

None can argue that 3's at their very best are a voice of reason, unafraid to speak up for the truth, and excellent at calling people to the carpet when they are taking advantage of others. A great scripture for a 3 to remember is found in Ephesians 4:15, which says we are called to *"speak the truth in love,"* as well as Proverbs 15:1, *"A soft answer turns away wrath."* When implemented, these words will be life-giving to family and friends that a 3 wants to have loyalty and longs to be truly loved and connected for just being themselves more than anything related to achievement. A 3 who exudes these traits becomes absolutely irresistible so that won't be hard!

If you are a 3, what are the gifts and superpowers you can be proud of? What tips will you take with you from this knowledge of self?

_____

_____

_____

_____

Type 4

Mary is a cosmetologist who is looking for someone who is able to grasp the complexity and depths of her compassionate and wounded soul. She fears being alone but values life's ideals, displaying beauty and detailed work at its finest.

4's find their pleasure by seeking and expressing beauty in the world. They are often called "The Idealist" or "The Romantic." They are compassionate and good at going to the dark, emotional places with people. They want real conversations and depth with others. Often 4's create various art forms for the world to fully understand or view as a lens to see God's beauty. 4's can be quite moody, jealous and sullen, looking at the grass on the other side as though it's so much greener and brighter than their own blessed, though different life.

Their relationship tendencies are to find someone that helps them to create an identity they feel is finally worthy of notice, which was somewhat muddled growing up for some reason or another. In health, 4's recognize that they didn't "miss the memo," that the grass is not always greener on the other side, that they are not inherently flawed or victims, that and they rest in bringing their intuitive beauty and deep compassion wherever they go.

Type 4's also have a deep sense of right and wrong. They are a safe place for those needing to process raw and misunderstood feelings. At their best, sensitive 4's find beauty even in painful circumstances instead of wallowing in self-pity. Their biggest work is reminding themselves that they are not *only* their hurt feelings and that they *can* choose to step outside of those into a healthier thought life.

They also must realize that they don't have to label themselves as unique and different to be worthy of love. They are already unique and deeply loved, and not irredeemably deficient. Instead of focusing on the missing tragic flaw they often feel is at the center of their person that disqualifies them from belonging in the world, they do well to focus on their rich and wild interior life, and to continue sitting with others in their pain. A 4 can express the depths they carry through art, activity, and healthy solitude where they can be reminded to *"take every thought captive to the obedience of Christ,"* (2nd Cor 10:5). They need to believe that they can choose to think more positively.

If you are a 4, what are the gifts and superpowers you can be proud of? What tips will you take with you from this knowledge of self?

_____

_____

_____

_____

Type 5

Jay is a researcher for a newspaper firm and his job includes long hours of study behind the scenes. He also works under a pseudonym as well. His favorite pastime activities after work are making graphic designs which he also does entirely behind the scenes. His family jokes as he comes out of his home office that he's been in his "bat cave."

5's are the researchers, often called, "The Investigators" of the Enneagram. They bring their gifts of intensely focusing on projects and pursuing brilliance and information of all types. They are also able to work and find enjoyment from the quiet recesses of their own minds. They are not *always* introverts but most 5's are, since they have limited energy or interest in conversations. They enjoy just settling back and watching at times, exploring, viewing the world in front of them or resting. By their bird's eye view, they learn a myriad of interesting facts and thereby when they do step into life, they offer vision and a ready wit to the world. They research and learn all they can till they not only discover but master as many things about the world as possible.

The self-sustenance of a 5 can be off-putting to would-be

pursuers of friendship or love. This complete self-reliance is often a defense since 5's are fearful of being overwhelmed and have been so in the past with fatigue or emotional troubles from others. They spend a lot of time thinking, which can take care of many of their needs, but 5's need to know that accessing feelings is important, too. At their best, a 5 can share their constant thirst and retention of knowledge with others and take needed introvert breaks for fulfillment, re-emerging when ready to share their wealth of knowledge, bravely putting fear aside and engaging with the world.

The high intelligence of a 5 can make them arrogant and highly annoyed with people, especially people who try to take them to places they don't want to go or don't follow their pre-planned scripts for how the 5 had imagined conversations would go.

5's like to be quite free, are able to do things independently and have wonderful focus. They love working alone on projects and can save money like nobody's business. Since they don't want to have to rely on anyone for anything, they rarely ask for their needs to be met. If a 5 does find someone worthy to take a risk on and to love, they will give up their time freely, deeply and liberally.

In contrast, when they feel overwhelmed and tired by the idea of having to give in too many places, they can present as shut off and emotionally distant. Communicating this bravely helps others to understand that it's truly anxiety-provoking to a 5 to share feelings and completely foreign, since it takes them a long time to access feelings. Give them time to do this, even if it takes a few days to mull over.

Thankfully, a healthy 5 will only retreat or withdraw long enough until it is safe to come out again, and their cup is once again overflowing. When a 5 needs to let go, a great verse for a 5 to meditate on, as they release trust to God, is 2 Corinthians 12:9, *"But he said to me, 'My grace is sufficient for you, for my power is made perfect in weakness.' Therefore I will boast all the more gladly of my weaknesses, so that the power of Christ may rest upon me."*

If you are a 5, what are the gifts and superpowers you can be proud of? What tips will you take with you from this knowledge of self?

Type 6

Jen was often worried about her family because she loved them so much. It was next to impossible to plan her surprise 40th birthday since she was suspiciously watching her husband's every move, knowing something was awry.

6's are guardians of their closest relationships, bringing their gift of creating security, courage and wisdom to their friendships and situations. They revel in being extremely loyal to their favorite people and in detailed contingency planning for all kinds of emergencies. A 6 is the man or woman on the plane with every possible medical supply in their carry-on or the man fluidly leading his team on workplace safety, since he's already thought through all possible emergency preparation steps himself as a natural coping mechanism.

A type 6, due to their anxiety, can be wary and distrustful of others. To combat this thread of insecurity, they link or merge with perceived safe authority figures, and thereby create multiple escape-hatch options for themselves. In some cases, instead of becoming anxious, a world-wary 6 can become counter-anxious (counterphobic) and defy or reject even healthy authorities and sources of wisdom, like the Bible. A counterphobic six may try to find security in substances or dangerous group activities as a temporary solution.

However, these kinds of counterproductive behaviors may cause a 6 to ironically lose credibility and even good relationships and experiences because of their fears. This downward spiral can be avoided by processing their fears safely, by grieving their losses, and by accessing logical tools, healthy emotional outlets, and by doing healthy bodywork. In health, the brave courage and generosity of a 6 to friends and those they serve, despite their fear, exceeds that of any other type.

A blessing and a struggle of loyal 6's is that they will find the problem or loophole with every plan. At their best however, they are the person who is prepared for every worst case scenario, who is always ready to help a friend, and who is willing to deal with their anxiety courageously so they don't have to live in fear. Those who are fortunate enough to have a healthy 6 as a friend will find a wise, loyal and trustworthy person.

Type 6's love to be safe and secure above all things. They are distrustful unless trust is strongly earned and even then may be doubtful and suspicious of the loyalty and trustworthiness of others. It's also important that 6's learn to stop checking with authority figures and learn to trust their own instincts and inherent wisdom that God has given them, as they seek Him. A 6 does well to remember the important verse in 1 Corinthians 12:8, *"For to one is given the word of wisdom through the Spirit, and to another the word of knowledge according to the same Spirit."*

If you are a 6, what are the gifts and superpowers you can be proud of? What tips will you take with you from this knowledge of self?

_____

_____

_____

_____

Type 7

Jessica loves to start her days early and end them late, trying to fit in varied and stimulating experiences. She avoids making firm plans just in case something else needed tending. Her fear of losing control always runs just underneath the bubbling, happy surface.

7's are the enthusiasts of the world, bringing their gift of joy with them to their families, friends and vocations. Their joy comes from within and without, from the everyday wonders in nature, from the beautiful and optimistic energy they often feel inside, and from their vivid imaginations, where they spend a lot of time taking care of their own emotional needs. Most 7's try to take care of their own emotional needs because they've learned long ago in childhood not to be a nuisance to others, and in some cases, learned that others are not always readily available for nurturing, especially since when a 7 gets anxious, they tend to need a lot of it.

7's also love ideas and new experiences, and because of their desire to be stimulated, often rooted in anxiety, they can be quite gluttonous with those activities.

Their challenge is they can flit from thing to thing, avoid finishing worthy projects, and try to avoid facing the deep feelings of life, endings, and anything they cannot reframe into a positive. They do this because they are afraid they will be in pain, alone and overwhelmed, and they will try to do anything to escape the anxiety of the unknown and difficult-to process-emotions. This is a decent short-term strategy for avoiding pain, but in the long run, if the pain is left unprocessed, it leaves a 7 holding up a lot of plates up, exhausted, scattered, and in more pain than they would have been in had they just processed it in the first place. Sometimes it even leaves them temporarily addicted to something that blocks their fears until it is processed and grieved.

A healthy 7 doesn't scatter but follows through and become focused on a strong finish. Endings are seen as accomplishments, as the 7 no longer views the completion of a task or race as a scary or negative event since they're managing their anxiety in better ways. They find that not only can they get through the pain and the unfinished business of life, but that they can also encourage others in their pain, and still share their joyous laughter wherever they go.

Although Type 7's love laughter, fun, exercise, new restaurants, high fashion, and pretty much "all the things!" a healthy seven who can embrace painful feelings can take it at a healthy pace, knowing they truly thrive when they get rest. As such, the home life of a healthy 7 can be very simple, and they may enjoy introverted time quite frequently to give their "energizer bunny battery" a reset.

If they don't sometimes let go of the bustling calendar of fun things in exchange for dealing with the hard things of life, all kinds of anxious gluttony can become a real vice. These include overeating, addictions, over exercising, overworking, and just overdoing in general. A 7 does well to remember Matthew 11:28 here, that God is available to listen to their pain and can offer solace and help even when a 7 is out of commission or overwhelmed with unpleasant emotions, Jesus says *"Come to me all you who are weary and burdened and I will give you rest."*

If you are a 7, what are the gifts and superpowers you can be proud of? What tips will you take with you from this knowledge of self?

_____

_____

_____

_____

Type 8

Rick is a proud Enneagram 8 and a lawyer. He wins many arguments in and out of court, and he lives every day to the fullest, protecting his family in the way he sees best. He admires strong global leaders even if he doesn't always agree with them. He is passionate about art and takes pride in being physically strong. He always gives it his all.

8's are the strong leaders of the world, often called, "The

Challengers," since they're wonderful at protecting themselves and others from the threats around them. Like 6's, they can sense a threat, but they will boldly take it down as well, on their own, if necessary.

An 8 in charge of a group will push others to their maximum capacity, defending and rooting for the perceived underdogs, whom they often consider their family members they have to protect at all costs. 8's forge bold paths, dauntless in the face of any given foe. At their best, they are fearless leaders, generals of families or armies, leading people into worthy battles and trusting a few people who have proved themselves, even forgiving those who have let them down in the past. At their worst they can be domineering, controlling and wild in anger, deceitful and lustful of all good things, overindulging.

8's don't seem to be afraid of just about anything or anyone, at least not on the surface. In fact, in the body triad which we'll talk about soon, the most easily reached limbic system response of an 8 is overt anger. No one is going to catch an unhealthy 8 being vulnerable about other emotions. Most 8's learned as a child that being vulnerable would not get them respect or take them to higher places of survival, often an important coping strategy for a child raised in a traumatic, difficult or rigid setting. It's not that they want to fight, it's just that their guard is up to boldly defend their causes and it's just not in their passionate nature to withdraw from a challenge.

People are so blessed to have a protective 8 to love them. The 8 has great energy, more than any other of the types typically, and will live life to the full. An 8 does well to remember that even if it isn't always wise to trust man, since they have often lost a lot of that due to their root issues, a loving and good God is available to help them through each and every trial. Their joy and passion will be balanced as they seek God and finally become vulnerable to Him. Psalm 118:8, "It is better to take refuge in the Lord than to trust in man."

If you are an 8, what are the gifts and superpowers you can be proud of? What tips will you take with you from this knowledge of self?

_____

_____

_____

_____

Type 9

Michelle is fun-loving and peaceful. When someone insulted her at work last week, she preferred to think about other things instead of dealing with it directly. She went home and baked, watched her favorite show and let the stress melt away as best as she could for the time being. She slept extra long that night and tried to avoid her rude coworker the next day.

The type 9's of the world are aptly called, "The Peacemakers," because they bring their gifts of offering calm and fun domesticity to the world. They have the most gentle, kind and unobtrusive ways possible, not asking others for more than is their share, and often deferring to them. A 9's core wound or issue is often reported as feeling that they weren't always seen or heard, whether through active trauma, or just having an overly busy parent, being a middle child in a large family, or perhaps not meshing with a parent's personality very well. At any rate, because of their defensiveness, they may naturally slide into the background in a group setting. That's a tragedy, not only because 9's miss out but because the rest of the world misses out on the bubbly, fun, truth-telling, peace, detail, and sharp wit of a magnetic and multi-talented 9.

In addition, 9's actually love being welcomed and included, most actually being very much extroverted at the core. When they're not in a lively routine or when they're not being heard, they can grow sleepy from sitting on unexpressed anger. At their worst, 9's can be lacking goals, vision, and narcotize to food, medications, and television since they don't feel like what they're doing has any focus or balance.

At their best they have the keen ability to feel what others are feeling on all sides of issues so they are able to be good diplomats, excellent teachers and amazing parents. Staying centered in their bodies and releasing anger in healthy manners are important steps for a 9. This often looks like making lists, building routines, and working out.

Because 9's do feel what others are feeling quite naturally, they aren't judgmental at all. This can lead them to be avoiders of conflict, sometimes forgetting that peace comes *through* conflict. When they show up for their life and choose healthy directions to go versus complacency and stagnation, they come back from the cave or turtle sleep of retreating in conflict. We tell 9's that it's OK to retreat for a half hour or up to two hours maximum, but to remember they are blessings to the world and have more true fun and lively living when they show up again. 9's exude naturally the scripture that it's good to consider one another as better than themselves in Phil 2:3, but they also do well to remember *"to love others as themselves"* (Matthew 22:39).

If you are a 9, what are the gifts and superpowers you can be proud of? What tips will you take with you from this knowledge of self?

_____

_____

_____

_____

As you reviewed each type carefully, we're sure you found that you had elements of many of the types, not just one. However, as we mentioned earlier, try to identify with one more than the others so you can focus on the growth tips for that type more than any other as well. We do our growing step by step, remember, and after you've succeeded in one area, you can feel free to move into the next. If we are healthy in all nine areas, we bring a more complete picture of a healthy and balanced individual and follower of Christ.

The Heart, Head, and Body Triads

Now that you've got your Enneagram type securely set, you can also take a moment to notice which way you react first, your head, your heart, or your gut. Type 2's, 3's, and 4's typically react first with their feelings or heart, Type 5's, 6's and 7's usually react first with their thinking or head, and Type 1's, 8's and 9's often react with their gut instincts about people, experiencing it in their bodies.

The Heart Triad

If you're in the heart triad, this is very positive in the sense that your heart can often tell motives very well, since accessing your heart is your superpower of sorts, allowing you to read others well. Since you also tend to react with shame when you're not in health, sometimes you react off of   feelings only, giving your power and even your very self to others too easily, neglecting thinking things through logically and often wisely. If you're a 2 you try to help the world to find your worth, as a 3 you try to earn your worth through work and achievements, and as a 4, you try to show the world you're invaluable because of your creative and different style.

Instead of falling naturally into this, the Bible said instead of trusting your heart on its own, *"Trust the Lord with all your heart, leaning not into your own understanding,"* in Proverbs 3:5. Try allowing wisdom and thinking into your strategies of getting healthy so you're not basing everything off of feelings, which will surely ebb and flow. Enjoy that the good parts of your heart help you some, but don't give it all the power. Jeremiah 17:9-10 says this, *"The heart is more deceitful than all else. And is desperately sick; Who can understand it? I, the LORD, search the heart, I test the mind."*

Let God help you think clearly and create in you a clean,

trusting heart toward Him first before you give it over to anyone else. Only He can fill it or satisfy it in the complete way, as He is your Maker and wants you to wisely follow Him before any person. He wants you to seek His approval, not theirs. As Matthew 6:33 says, *"But seek ye first the kingdom of God, and his righteousness; and all these things shall be added unto you."*

What do you think God means when He said when you seek Him first, all these things will be added to you?

_____

_____

_____

_____

What do you think God means when He says we cannot fully trust the heart?

_____

_____

_____

_____

How can you let your heart and instincts guide you but also personally start thinking things through more logically? In our experience, getting things out of the heart (in imagination, child brain) and into the spoken or written form (adult, real world), helps quite a bit. If you're in the heart triad, what will you do to strengthen your mind?

_____

_____

_____

_____

The Head Triad

If you're in the thinking/head triad, you typically experience reactive thoughts before anything else typically. Since I (Christa) am in this triad, I can think of an emergency within a moment's notice, and I'm already picturing how to respond with my mind. I am thinking it all through and the thoughts are sometimes stressful and create anxiety. As a 7, I could reframe then to temporarily push all negative thoughts away. If I were a 6, I would find a way to secure myself, and if I were a 5, I would try to reduce my possibility of feeling things by pushing away from everyone and seeking inner knowledge to help me through.

Better than allowing only these temporary fixes, those of us in the thinking triad need to face our fears, like a 6 often does, but instead of only trying to create security (which this world cannot always give), we need to seek God for peace, pouring out our disappointments to Him through accessing our feelings as well. Contrary to 2's, 3's and 4's who are great at examining the feelings of others and themselves (3's struggle on the latter), the head triad member thinkers often leave the heart out altogether and become very mechanical or slower at grieving something that needs to be dealt with. They need to be reminded that as long as they don't give feelings full power, even if feelings don't feel very practical to express, it's very healthy to allow them in for a short time.

They may even allow themselves five minutes a day to not only think of or worry about, but to *process* negative feelings through writing, speaking or crying. Then fear is decreased and joy, wisdom, and focus will be renewed more wholly, and not in scattered or sinful ways. The Bible verse 1 Peter 5:7, is a great one to remember. *"Cast all your anxiety on him because he cares for you."* Your mind needs a release, through emotions and also through the body. Workouts help in this latter aspect, and there are many studied that can concur working out helps people to process difficult emotions also.

How can you let your thoughts and instincts guide you but also personally start allowing God to heal your heart as well, trusting in Him? In our experience, letting it out with a safe person like a counselor or coach is a good place to start, as is a private journal where you can reflect and release. If you're in the head triad, what will you do to release your fears?

_____

_____

_____

_____

The Body Triad

The final triad is the anger or body / gut triad. If you're in this anger triad, as a 1, 8, or 9, you experience frustration first, even if you don't always tell others about it. If you're a 1 or a 9 however, you don't really even feel like admitting to yourself and others that you're stressed and angry. Perhaps you weren't given attention or you thought anger was an unhealthy emotion that should be concealed. At any rate, it does need expression, just not all the time.

As a 9, you get tired or sleepy, narcotizing the pain through TV or food. As a type 8 you prepare to meet the challenge with your anger directly. No one will find you vulnerable to it, even though sometimes you do need to temper it. If you're a 1, you repress anger, a "bad" emotion, and you don't let anyone see it till the anger is thick or you're so angry it comes out as passive or active rage.

Those in the body triad do well to remember that instead of letting your gut instinct provide you with ALL of the information about what's right and wrong, try to allow your thoughts to logically slow you down and to create a truer color picture than just a simple black and white photo. Add color by considering other people's gifts that differ from yours or their trauma, and perhaps remembering the gratitude you have.

Accessing your heart is also huge, as is showing your true and unguarded feelings to a few safe people regularly. You are so strong and guarded from hurts, but you too need *healthy* releases (remember 8's release but need healthy ways of doing it), and the people in your life need to see your heart not just your anger, which even if you think it doesn't show (9's and 1's), it does. Since you store and react to stress in the body, working out, massage, or whatever other meditative or helpful bodywork you enjoy is so critical for your release and success. In Jesus' culture, people could walk and work their feelings out more naturally, whereas now our only exercise, if we desire, is finger exercises on our phones as we work from home, order take out, and drive in automatic cars.

A great verse to remember that will help you to express more openly, and not repress things till you burst in sin, overdo, or become numb is this, *"Do you not know that your bodies are temples of the Holy Spirit, who is in you, whom you have received from God? You are not your own; you were bought at a price. Therefore honor God with your bodies."* This is found in 1 Corinthians 6:19-20. Take care of your whole body, including your heart and your mind as well.

How can you let your instinct and gut responses guide you but also personally start allowing God to heal your heart as well, trusting in Him and opening your heart to people who have proven to be safe, though imperfect? In our experience, letting your bodily stress out in a safe format also helps, as does sharing things with a safe person, such as a Type 2 who will listen with love. If you're in the body triad, what will you do to release your stress?

_____

_____

_____

_____

After that thorough analysis, you definitely know about your type, but knowing is only half the battle. Allow the Holy Spirit to transform and to guide your thought life, heart, and behaviors. Here are some great strategies for staying near the healthier side of yourself depending on whatever type you are:

Type 1: Good therapy or stress reducing techniques: Reading the

Reading the Serenity prayer (by Reinhold Niebuhr), going outdoors on a nature walk and noticing "imperfections" are part of the changing seasons, learning to set boundaries on workload, bodywork, resisting being a critical inner voice to self and inner/outer to other people, adding fun and an encouraging inner and outer voice more along with far less value judgements.

Type 2: Good therapy or stress reducing techniques: Trying not to rescue everyone all the time, not giving just to get or keeping even. In your accomplishments, being proud but humble, avoiding seduction, codependency, or friendship manipulation as tools to getting needs met, clear forthright discussions, God esteem and self care. Using your thought life to guide you, talk to the Holy Spirit versus just sitting in your own feelings.

Type 3: Good therapy or stress reducing techniques: Finding happiness within yourself versus a partner, finding someone who loves you for things other than just your achievements, finding friends who will encourage you to have fun and relax but also not force you away from your competitive job and lifestyle too much. Avoid deceit and control, be softer, speak the truth in love, apologize after being harsh, access sad feelings for a few minutes a day. Release, don't give in all the time to a mate like a chameleon but be proudly you.

Type 4: Good therapy or stress reducing techniques: Allow your art to bring beauty to your life and don't expect others to meet all of those needs. Balancing your introvert and extrovert needs, trying to not judge and remembering God loves you when jealousy stirs, allowing bodywork and thought life to temper your passionate anger, not allowing feelings to totally lead, apologizing as needed with sincerity and patience.

Type 5: Good therapy or stress reducing techniques: Work on fewer projects more in depth and focused, allowing safe others in regularly, but not everyone. When energy permits, seek knowledge but then bravely putting it to work, risking healthy relationships, reducing fantasy and overthinking, giving your

111

mind breaks through meditation, moderate exercise and releasing of feelings.

Type 6: Good therapy or stress reducing techniques: Access your heart not just thoughts, checking on paranoid thoughts logically before sabotaging relationships or becoming rebellious against the good to "protect" yourself, scheduling in a limited time to worry versus letting it run your schedule, working out to get a mind break, Bible memory about fear and courage, helping others through their fears, not avoiding healthy risk but planning healthy security and then completing your goals, not controlling or nitpicking others because of your own struggles.

Type 7: Good therapy or stress reducing techniques: Exercise, saving the fun for rewards after hard work increments, sticking to one or two bigger ventures a year versus scattering and not completing, being present and staying in the moment of activity or emotional connection and enjoying it, kinetic learning sometimes but also sitting and focusing as needed with music or touch, hot baths or showers, moderate eating and activity versus gluttony, acknowledging that pain will not kill you and is part of life.

Type 8: Good therapy or stress reducing techniques: Trusting safe (though imperfect) people somewhat and increasingly with time, actively telling the people closest to you that you want to retreat when they hurt you because you love them and that your protection is because you love them, bodywork, caring not control, being self-controlled versus gluttonous, kind and not demanding, trusting God versus following your gut that says you have to control man to be safe.

Type 9: Good therapy or stress reducing techniques: Making lists that keep you moving and on a healthy path, staying present in the body, addressing important issues of anger when it's an area of "right action" or very important to you, making sure you repeat yourself until heard, don't give up. Stay in the body, when anxiety hits, use it as momentum or do exercise or express your pain to release it. Not everyone will listen the first time, don't give up, you're worth it.

So now that you're trying to actively be at your best, who can you ask to both love you and hold you accountable on the journey? Perhaps you can find a mentor, a discipleship partner, a Bible study group, or your spouse or a counselor. Find someone who loves you and your family, and believes that you can and will grow, as well as offers you grace! Sharon and I see clients and make many specialized referrals to other helpful clinicians within our network, so please reach out if you're in need. Our contact info is in the back of the book! :)

Name the person or or a few people you'd like to reach out to about this. Check in with them now via text, email, or phone! If they can't try the next person on the list!

_____

_____

AFTERWORD

Congratulations! You've completed the awesome journey of exploring how God made you to thrive. You may be a female-brained, choleric, middle child, Enneagram 3 who loves acts of service and also dancing the Macarena. You may have discovered that you're a firstborn, Type 2 with a 3 wing, sanguine-supine like Sharon or a last born, Type 7 who goes to 5 in health, sanguine-choleric like Christa. Whatever your gifts and type, one of the most important things you can take from this book is that you are you, indefinitely unique and wonderfully made by the God who deeply loves you.

We hope this book is exactly what you needed to revive and to thrive in your gifts and relationships. In these ten modules, we've helped you to build a strong relationship foundation, recognizing ways you can thrive as you develop your own gifts and self care as well as maturely grow together as a connected couple.

We've shared God's amazing plan for even the broken pieces of your life both in your weaknesses and even in finding ways your traumas can be reclaimed. You've learned how to become healthily interdependent and to have fun together versus just being clingy, abusive or otherwise codependent, overly focused on your mate for meeting all attachment needs.

We've also explored wonderful and unique you! We looked at you through the lens of a myriad of typology angles, including male versus female brain patterns, love languages, birth order, temperaments and Enneagram.

We hope that now that your brain is full of great information, you will use these tools we've given you for a fun, full and lasting marriage, one that displays the confident, interdependent, fun, and interesting person God made you to be. This is the way you can truly thrive.

As we close, however, we want to leave you with one final reminder and that cannot be overstated.

The single most important piece of relationship success is each individual's relationship with God. Yes, we each bring our uniqueness and gifts to the table, but it is God's opinion of us that matters, for He is our Maker, and as St. Augustine once said, *"You have made us for Yourself, O Lord, and our heart is restless until it rests in You."* Only God has the full power and ability to give us courage, to heal our wounds, and to forgive us from our sins, once and for all, despite our continued weaknesses. Have you asked Jesus into your heart? Have you asked Him to forgive you and to be Lord over your life?

In Joseph's story in the Bible, you learn that when you turn over your life to God, (what the enemy means for evil) in Genesis 50:20, God will always turn into His glory. However, God is no more a vending machine to be sought out only as a surface level relationship any more than your spouses and family should be treated as a mere mechanism.

God invites us into constant fellowship with Himself. When asked how we can inherit eternal life with Him, Jesus answered, *"Love the Lord your God with all your heart and with all your soul and with all your strength and with all your mind'; and, 'Love your neighbor as yourself."* This is found in Luke 10:27.

He wants us to work out our relationships issues and not to keep our heart, body, or mind from Him. He wants it all, and only then, when fully surrendered to Him, can we really love those we closely relate to in the very best ways.

Don't fear as you surrender. God will ultimately give you double for your troubles. Remember, as we learn in Isaiah 61, Jesus came to bind up your broken heart and to heal your past hurts and challenges. Use this book and more importantly, the book of all books, the Bible, as a courageous reminder to make your marriage as wonderful as possible and to be what you cannot be alone. The reward will be great.

If you need support, find someone to help you walk through your differences and allow the Holy Spirit to help you on your journey. Our trials will have a specific purpose, and we will able to help others with the same comfort we receive, as we learn in 2nd Corinthians 1:3-4, *"Praise be to the God and Father of our Lord Jesus Christ, the Father of compassion and the God of all comfort, who comforts us in all our troubles, so that we can comfort those in any trouble with the comfort we ourselves receive from God."*

Who will you ask to keep you accountable and fully supported as you walk this journey of reviving and thriving in your gifts and relationships?

_____

_____

_____

_____

Thank you so much to our clients and those who have shared their stories and dreams with us. Thank you especially to our spouses who have given us the gift of marriage so that we too have someone to help us up when we fall, to enjoy, and with which to grow. And thank you to you, dear reader, for sharing the journey with us. It is a privilege to bear the secrets of others so they too can bring the dark into the light to advance the gospel.

ABOUT THE AUTHORS

Christa Hardin, M.A. Relationship Coach

My job is my dream vocation and my calling. I started helping couples when I was just a kid, counseling my friends and typing in notes while they lay on my bed. I also gave my parents advice, sending notes back and forth for them under the door or trying to arbitrarily calm them from the backseat when they had a fight. I later went to grad school in Psychology at Wheaton College, where I learned to integrate faith with practice. I'm at home with my kids part-time as a homeschool teacher, and I run my practice Reflections Counseling & Coaching in Southwest Florida, which I began in 2012. I've written devotionals and Bible studies for several audiences as well as the R & R Marriage Series for couples. Besides work, my joys are my family, writing, working out, nature, skiing (a rare treat!) and reading. I can be reached @ **Christa@ReflectionsCC.com**

Sharon Otis, Ph.D., Psychologist

I started my career teaching with a commitment to children and families fifty years ago. The commitment took me to earn several master degrees in special education, school counseling, school psychology and even school administration. In this journey to reach children in the most effective way, I learned that I must work with the whole family to affect change. The relationship each parent has with each other is the foundation for children to learn to cope with life. Helping the parents relate to each other and bring them into a loving, personal relationship with Jesus is now my mission in this next phase if my life. I can be reached @ **Docsotis@aol.com**   I also have books on parenting on Amazon and Kindle in English and Spanish.

NOTES

Introduction & Module 1

No non-biblical references. All Scripture quotations, unless otherwise indicated, are taken from the Holy Bible, New International Version®, NIV®. Copyright ©1973, 1978, 1984, 2011 by Biblica, Inc. The "NIV" and "New International Version" are trademarks registered in the United States Patent and Trademark Office by Biblica, Inc. Several Scripture quotations are taken from the New American Standard Bible®, Copyright © 1960, 1962, 1963, 1968, 1971, 1972, 1973, 1975, 1977, 1995 by The Lockman Foundation. (www.Lockman.org)

J.R.R. Toklien, *The Return of the King*, 2012 Del Ray Mass Market Edition.

Module 2

No non-biblical references.

Module 3

www.npr.org May 2, 2015, https://www.npr.org/sections/health-shots/2015/03/02/387007941/take-the-ace-quiz-and-learn-what-it-does-and-doesnt-mean

Module 4

https://www.psychologytoday.com/us/blog/the-theory-cognitive-modes/201405/left-brain-right-brain-two-sides-always-working-together

https://www.google.com/amp/s/www.psychologytoday.com/us/blog/hope-relationships/201402/brain-differences-between-genders%3famp

https://www.google.com/amp/s/www.psychologytoday.com/us/blog/abcs-child-psychiatry/201605/are-brains-male-or-female%3famp

https://www.google.com/amp/s/www.psychologytoday.com/us/articles/201711/the-truth-about-sex-differences%3famp

Module 5

University of Georgia psychologist Alan E. Stewart wrote what is perhaps the definitive recent work (2012) on the theory and research on birth order. He bases his paper on 529 journal articles published over a 20-year period. (The sheer number of studies on birth order is a testimony to the importance of this topic in psychology.) https://www.psychologytoday.com/us/blog/fulfillment-any-age/201305/is-birth-order-destiny

The Five Love Languages: Secrets to Love That Lasts by Gary D. Chapman, Northfield Publishing, Chicago, 2015

His Needs, Her Needs: Building an Affair-Proofing Marriage by Willard F. Harley, Jr. , Revell Publishing, 2011

Module 6

Confessions by Saint Augustine, Oxford University Press, Translation and Notes, Henry Chadwick, 1991

The Bible app is found at www.YouVersion.com

Module 7

No non-biblical references.

Module 8

No non-biblical references.

Module 9

https://www.psychologytoday.com/us/blog/the-worlds-within-our-minds/201702/how-temperament-impacts-entrepreneurship

https://www.psychologytoday.com/us/blog/short-history-mental-health/201311/balancing-your-humors

Boundaries by Dr. Henry Cloud and Dr. John Townsend, published by Zondervan, 2017

www.temperamentquiz.com

Module 10 & Afterword

Enneagram watercolor chart done by Amanda Dodson of Dodson Designs.

The Enneagram test falls under common use. General information about the Enneagram can be found at www.enneagraminstitute.com

https://www.yourenneagramcoach.com/p/yecassessment

The Serenity Prayer by Reinhold Niebuhr, used in AA also.

Confessions by Saint Augustine, Oxford University Press, Translation and Notes, Henry Chadwick, 1991

Made in the USA
Columbia, SC
26 September 2023

23414475R00079